Searching Out Loud: Giving Voice to Independent Investigations

Searching Out Loud

Giving Voice to Independent Investigations

A Digital Media and Information Literacy Curriculum for Reporters, Researchers, and Legal Professionals

UNIT FOUR:

How to Focus on Information Context, Including Misinformation

Copyright © 2019 Marc Solomon

All rights reserved. No part of this book may be reproduced in any form or by any electronic or mechanical means, including information storage and retrieval systems, without permission in written form from the publisher, except for reviewers, who may quote brief passages in a review.

ISBN (978-1-7332554-9-3) print version
ISBN (978-1-7332554-5-5) e-book version

Some characters and events in this book are fictitious. Any similarity to real persons, living or dead, is coincidental and not intended by the author.

Promotion of the books, tools, applications, and creative works of...
  Romantic Deception by Dr. Sally Caldwell and Darlene E. Adams
  Finding Birthdays and Related Persons in One Step by Stephen P. Morse
  SurfWax search engine by Tom Holt
  Gigablast search engine by Matt Wells
  L-Soft and LISTSERV® trademark by L-Soft International, Inc.
  SearchEngineLand by ThirdDoorMedia.com
  WorldCat image and trademark by OCLC.org
  BRB Public Records by BRB Publications, LLC

Reprinted by permission.

Book Design by Davin Pasek and Emma Koramshahi of Paradise Copies
All photographs by the author unless otherwise credited.

Printed and bound in USA
First Printing September 2019

Published by The Society of Useful Information
4 French Street
Hadley, MA 01035

Visit www.searchingoutloud.org

For Patty, who taught me the root of all source knowledge:
Enduring gratitude

"I was gratified to be able to answer promptly, and I did. I said I didn't know."

— **Mark Twain**

"The most courageous act is still to think for yourself. Aloud."

— **Coco Chanel**

"No provider or user of an interactive computer service shall be treated as the publisher or speaker of any information provided by another information content provider."

— **Communications Decency Act, Section 230**

Searching Out Loud
Giving Voice to Independent Investigations

CURRICULUM GUIDE c:1
    Knowledge-Enabled Digital Literacy Curriculum and Book Structure
        UNIT ONE: How to Project Manage Virtual Investigations c:1
        UNIT TWO: Using Search in Virtual Investigations c:3
        UNIT THREE: How to Source Information that Instructs c:6
        UNIT FOUR: Focusing on Information Context **c:9**
        UNIT FIVE: How to Present What We Learn in Teachable Ways c:12
        UNIT SIX: The Knowledge-ABLED Cookbook c:15

UNIT FOUR: Focusing on Information Context **4:1**
    SECTION 4.0: Focusing on Information Context 4:1
        Taken into Context 4:1
        Stumbling into Context 4:1
        Unit Four Learning Objectives 4:2
        Unit Four Benefits 4:5
    SECTION 4.1: Individual-based Information 4:7
        Personal Motivation 4:7
        Introducing Provider Conjugation Frameworks 4:8
        The Three Type of Information Exchanges 4:11
        Containers of Information Exchanges within Groups 4:12
        Provider Conjugation: Individual and Group Motivation Vectors 4:14
        Individual: Second Person 4:16
        Individual: Third Person 4:17
        Group Behavior in Provider Conjugation 4:19
        Group: First Party 4:20
        Group: Second Party 4:23
        Group: Third Party 4:26
        Credibility as Social Dynamic 4:33
        Sourcing Credible References 4:35
        Lateral Thinking as a Credibility Check 4:35
        Analyzing Context: The Vectors of Integrity 4:38
        Integrity Vectors 4:41
        The Verdict on Vectors 4:46
    SECTION 4.2: The Value of Social Information 4:47
        Using PCF to Render Radar Screens 4:48
        Authenticity, Credibility, Conflicts of Interest 4:49
        Working Under the Radar 4:52
    SECTION 4.3: Search to Converse 4:58
        Networking: How to Socialize What We Learn 4:58
        SOCIAL NETS: From Soul Searching to Online Searching 4:59
        The Concept of Social Circles 4:60
        SOCIAL NETS: From Searching to Conversing 4:63
        Build It – and They Will Dump 4:69
        Search to Converse 4:74
        Determining Your Online Identity 4:77

Social Bookmarking: Somebody Knows the Sites I've Seen	4:80
SECTION 4.4: Misinformation as an Information Source	4:87
Misinformation – When Context Disappears	4:87
The Limited Perspectives of Information Providers	4:87
Overcome by Events (and Misinformants)	4:96
Scoring Systems that Rate Themselves	4:104
The Dubious Freedom of Anonymous Speech	4:107
UNIT Four: Wrapping	
Focusing on Information Context	4:107

CURRICULUM GUIDE

Here is the structure used for organizing the book along with the chapters for delivering the methods and skills for becoming Knowledge-ABLED through the Searching Out Loud digital literacy curriculum.

===

UNIT ONE:
How to Turn Information into Knowledge
Preparing:
How to Project Manage Virtual Investigations

===

UNIT ONE SUMMARY

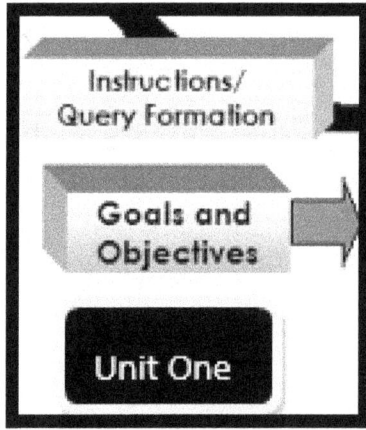

Our first section addresses search project management ("SPM"). SPM is based on the simple and often overlooked reality that being online costs a great deal; not in connect charges or even subscription fees but just by the shear amount of time we invest in searching, often with little to show for it.

Regardless of leaps in processing power, portability, and media convergence, there will remain a single problem reducible to two perennial questions: (1) what kinds of information are out there; and (2) how can what I'm looking for explain or even shape the decisions and actions I'll be making or revising?

SPM contains the discipline and focus that transcends technological change. In **Unit One** we apply SPM principles to recurring research assignments by setting out our information goals. To do this, we'll begin by defining what separates high from low quality information in pursuit of our project objectives. Then we'll decide on the appropriate research approach to our mission-specific projects. Finally, SPM gives us the focus to manage our search projects effectively so that the time and effort we invest is in line with the results we get online.

Searching Out Loud: Curriculum Guide and Book Structure | c:2

UNIT ONE SECTION STRUCTURE

1.1 Search Project Management: How do we assess what we want from our research sessions before we log into them

    a. How information becomes useful knowledge in pursuit of project goals and search targets

    b. An overview of the digital discovery process from initial exploration to knowledge mapping and informed decision-making

1.2 Search Logs: How do we document the successes and failures of our research according to the goals and objectives of our investigations

- Pursuing search targets with discipline through selective documentation and action-based questions

1.3 Blindspots: What are some common traps and limitations that impede independent investigations and our effectiveness as researchers

- Setting our information radar to gauge the awareness levels and blindspots of our search targets

1.4 Becoming Knowledge-ABLED: What is our role in bridging the divide between the communities we serve and the technologies that serve us as researchers

    a. What do search engines do and how do they work

    b. How search engines process information, where they get their processing, and how we can get them to do our bidding

Unit One Benefits

- Learn and adopt SPM – A step-by-step process that helps us take control of Internet searches
- Set goals, milestones, and resource limits for finding and applying pertinent information to our research projects
- Build information radars that reveal where our search targets are spending their time and attention and where they're distracted or unaware (blindspots)
- Identify the culprits that steal time from our virtual investigations so we can bypass them when they next arise
- Figure in the time and expense we save by applying sound site selection practices
- Calculate the value accrued in billing for our research services

Unit One Tables

- The Knowledge Continuum – The challenge of using the web for research
- Search Project Management steps and examples - Putting our cards on the table through search logs
- Example search logs – Travel agents, caregivers, criminal investigators
- Google search trade-offs for researchers - Working within search engine limitations

UNIT TWO:
How to Search for Information That Informs
Seeking:
Using Search in Virtual Investigations

UNIT TWO SUMMARY

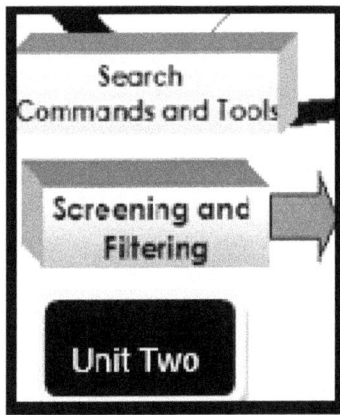

Unit Two is about tossing out the Driver's Ed instruction manual, getting in the car, and taking our established interests and new skills out for a test drive. **Unit Two** applies what we've learned about how search works to different engine and directory options. The goal is to conduct sophisticated, time-effective searches with a minimum of preparation and fees. Our priority is to focus on the best available tool and search strategy for the job at hand.

Having looked under the search engine hood in **Unit One**, we'll focus on tool selection, query formation, and refinement. We'll differentiate and select the right digital search and discovery tools, including visualization, cluster and NLP engines, as well as automated and human-filtered subject directories.

Next we start our meaningful exchanges with these tools by building effective queries. This means using the right search commands and word selection options for leveraging Internet resources, using correct syntax and semantics to express ourselves, and applying fact- and opinion-based guidelines to create productive outcomes.

Finally we draw on search operators, unique IDs, and pointers to either generalize or specify around the topics or our search targets – those events, policies, procedures, groups, or people in question. Our choices will depend not only on how but where we set our sights in the form of site selection.

Unit Two Section Structure

2.1 Query Formation: How to arrange, express, generalize, and specify our research questions

    a. What's a fair question and how to interview a search engine

    b. Conveying our intentions through syntax and search operators

    c. Refinements and corrections through term expansion and contraction

2.2 Semantics: What are the best terms for conducting research

    a. The role of informed word choice for building intentionality into search statements

    b. Applying unique IDs and verbatims to exact match and people searches

2.3 Tool Selection: What research tool to use and for which job

    a. Determining the right digital search and discovery tools for the questions we're raising, including visualization, cluster, metasearch and NLP engines

    b. Deciding on the right reference tools and recognized authorities in the fields we're searching including social media, portals, and subject directories

    c. Working with search engines, subject directories, or specialty databases when it's generalities, specifics, or somewhere in-between

2.4 Site Selection: Searching beyond search engines

    a. Where to do research and why size and location matters

    b. Determining the best starting point for the task at-hand

    c. Adjusting our approach to fit our resources

Unit Two Benefits

- Pose productive questions with a bias towards action
- Recognize appropriate search commands and word selection options for leveraging Internet resources
- Arrange and express effective search queries by using correct syntax and semantics
- Yield productive outcomes by applying fact- and opinion-based searches
- Generalize or specify around our topics and search targets by drawing on search operators, unique IDs, and pointers
- Overcome common pitfalls including familiar search detours, poor indexing, and character limits
- Reshape a misinformed question by redirecting our focus to more common problem sets and suggested searches

Unit Two Tables

- Defining what matters – The secret sauce of ordering search results through keywords, repetition, verbatims, and proximity
- Overcoming search limits – What we need to teach the search engine that it can't possibly know
- The haystacks and icebergs framework – Learning cues for opinion and fact-based searches
- Dialoging with search results through SEO (search engine optimization), unique IDs and pointers
- Answers, not documents – Defining natural language search engines
- Overlay of engines and directories – Precision versus recall

UNIT THREE:
How to Source Information That Instructs
Sourcing:
How to Evaluate Information Quality

UNIT THREE SUMMARY

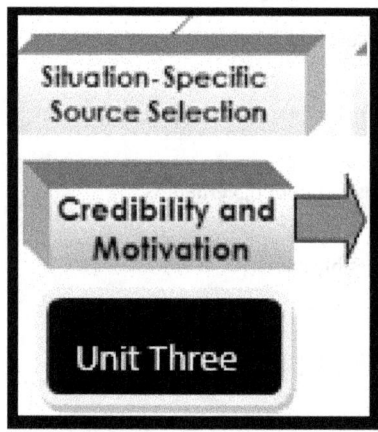

Unit Three focuses on acquiring source fluency and learning how to leverage those sources to improve the quality of the information you source virtually. The Unit starts by confronting the essential form of how information is delivered to us and the questions it inspires: Where is it located? What is it called? When was it done? Who did it? Why do I care? How do I find it again?

We can't possibly know everything and this is no less true for sourcing the world's knowledge. Committing an inventory of leading references and go-to experts on any subject is too daunting even for the reference librarians. Our goal is not to become librarians but to develop a skill called source fluency. Source fluency ensures that we're looking in the right place – even when we're a first-time visitor to unfamiliar topics. We'll set up a quality control process that not only reduces the search noise that clutters our screens. It also helps us to attract, analyze, and interpret the sources we need to fulfill our project objectives. We'll develop the quality of our findings on three levels: Search sets, websites, and individual pages (but only the ones worth opening)!

Unit Three is also devoted to unlocking the secrets, pitfalls and potentials of searching topic-focused Internet databases. Building on our **Unit Two** understanding of search engines (oceans) and subject directories (lakes), we'll dive into the information pond of more narrow and targeted specialty databases to uncover scarce and often overlooked information. OLP ("Oceans, Lakes, and Ponds") is the primary method for establishing: (1) source fluency, and (2) for determining *when* to pursue *what size* database in our virtual investigations.

UNIT THREE SECTION STRUCTURE

3.1 Information Types: How to integrate search findings into a useful form

    a. Surviving the search results page

    b. How information gets packaged in four dimensions – Entry-based, resource-based, view-based, and form-based

3.2 Source Fluency: How to cast our search nets for building source credibility and confidence

    a. Applying the concept of OLP ("Oceans, Lakes, and Ponds") to source the web

    b. Developing source fluency so we can apply sound sourcing methods no matter who's supplying the content

    c. How far to push and how deep to dig before drawing conclusions or reaching out to others

3.3 Quality Control: How to evaluate Information

    a. The three levels of quality control for skimming and assessing results sets, websites, and individual pages

    b. Determining when to use what source, including premium (fee-based) information and deep web (a.k.a. 'invisible web') sources

3.4 Managing Project Resources: How to price information's time and money dimensions

    a. Sizing up free versus fee – When it makes sense to use premium content and where to find it for minimal cost

    b. Using content groupings and specialty collections to narrow in on specifics or expand on topics

Unit Three Benefits

- Use appropriate techniques to analyze, interpret, and attract the sources you need to fulfill search objectives
- Regulate information quality – Focusing exclusively on sources worthy of our review
- Conduct an editorial check to qualify web-based publications
- Formulas to qualify resources, quantify our confidence in them, and avert the need to open individual pages
- Recognize where the likely boundary lies between public and proprietary information
- Know and apply the rules for uncovering overlooked information
- Reap the benefits of grouping sources for justifying our source choices
- Determine when the media becomes the story and not just the source of it

Unit Three Tables

- Quantity controls for testing the waters – Ratio of key indicators including the Google sniff test, and signal-to-noise formulas
- Link analysis for understanding the scope and reach of information providers
- The deep versus the shallow web – Why two Internets
- The media dietary chain – Recognizing source self-interest
- Using premium databases for climbing out of an information ditch

UNIT FOUR:
Sense-making:
Focusing on Information Context

UNIT FOUR SUMMARY

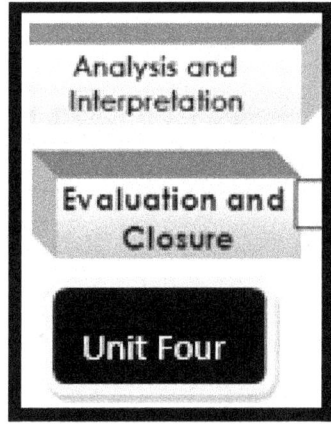

Unit Four has two principle thrusts: (1) Approaching research social networks as a researcher; and (2), engaging them as a member, including how to screen, join, attract, and communicate through virtual communities.

The slippery distinction between observer and participant is especially sensitive as we shift from the 'searching' to 'conversing" phase of our research projects. This section focuses on ways to trail and gather background details on search targets that generate digital identities through their social media profiles, networks, and commentary.

The model we use for reading networks and acting on them is called provider conjugation. Like verb conjugation, this tool helps to establish the flow and context of how information travels and the perceptions it carries with it. We also apply it to ourselves as information providers in determining the perceptions we want to form about us. This includes the types of contacts we want to attract and build into our own networks – especially in reaching out to search targets that prove to be social media party animals, digital hermits, or somewhere in-between.

Unit Four Section Structure

4.1. Provider Conjugation: How to determine the motives of information providers in groups and as individuals

    a. Defining senders, recipients and audiences to understand the direction and speed that information travels

    b. Assessing the nature and trade-offs of individuals and groups as information sources

    c. Leveraging lateral thinking as a tool for conducting Internet research

4.2 Misinformation as an information source: How to use information rather than *be used* by it

    a. Taking the sniff test to grounded or unfounded suspicions

    b. Decoding the role that gatekeepers, watchdogs, and regulators play in scandal-making

    c. Picking up the scent of smoking guns – Red flag conditions for conflicts of interest

    d. Opinions online – How to know who is gaming the system or fabricating their credentials

4.3 The value of social information: Applying provider conjugation to social media

    a. Using social bookmarking to vet source experts

    b. Trapping information through RSS feeds to target new opportunities

    c. Building custom search applications to uncover key details

    d. Gaining media cachet through blogging and selective interviewing

    e. Joining a professional network, cultivating contacts

4.4 Search to Converse: How to get from reading about others to direct engagement

    a. The giant listening ear as a networking asset

    b. Bartering information among groups and individuals

Unit Four Benefits

- Background research the people you're going to meet – Deploy specialized search tools to gauge their web presence and digital identities
- Build a stable of advisers and referral networks for finding experts and second opinions
- Assess the differences between the way information is communicated informally through word-of-mouth and institutionally through groups
- Apply the Vectors of Integrity to determine the credibility of information providers and their own involvement in the issues they report
- Gauge the reputation of our search targets (it's not in the eye of the beholder)!
- Leverage social networking tools to raise our digital profile as an independent investigator
- Use alerts and notifications to stay on top of fluid and evolving situations
- Pick a blog theme that can be strengthened by our research

Unit Four Tables

- Social Networks – From soul searching to role seeking
- Using link analysis to determine social circles
- Common tagging concepts for breaking new ground and reclaiming past breakthroughs
- The Seven Vectors of Relationship Integrity – Using online communities to weigh objective and subjective-based experience
- Credibility Pyramid – The scale of public scrutiny
- Cultivating contacts – Defining boundaries and fail-safes

UNIT FIVE:
How to Present What We Learn in Teachable Ways
Presenting:
How to Connect What You Learn to Useful Outcomes

Unit Five Summary

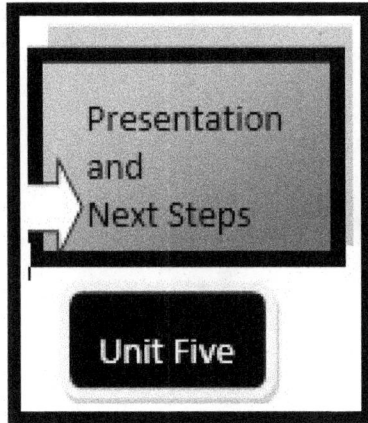

We talk about opportunities when we use information. We think in terms of risk when others do so. **Unit Five** focuses not only on what we learn but how this works in relation to what others know and perceive. How can we as messengers assess the nerves we strike and the buttons we push in the research we're delivering?

The first four units focus on how to gather information and act on it. **Unit Five** is about how others will act on the research we deliver through social media and more formal, offline channels: The reports and presentations to peers, clients, and groups (our "audience"). How will our findings be interpreted and acted on? How we deliver them is every bit as important as the research itself.

Unit Five brings together the search project management steps, query formation, quality controls, source fluency and information conjugation methods to deliver your research to the clients, colleagues, and communities we're supporting. These message receivers will clearly see how your informed use of web research tools and practices is bringing value, economy, and even closure to complex and resource-hungry investigations. We will then turn our attention to the report itself, coming to grips with the news we're delivering, the explanatory power of our analysis, and the changes we're proposing.

Unit Five Section Structure

5.1 Message Delivery: How to Knowledge-ENABLE our colleagues, clients and community through our findings, analysis, reporting, and recommended actions

    a. Confirmable Outcomes – Reducing uncertainty, building consensus, and making reasonable assertions from complex and resource-hungry investigations

    b. Results Verification –- *Closing the loop* between the words and deeds as well as the facts and opinions documented through our search logs

5.2 Information Packaging: Bringing together the SPM structure, query formation, source fluency, and information conjugation to deliver winning reports

    a. Packaging the results – What they should contain, what to leave out, and how they should unfold as a learning narrative

    b. Assimilating search results, coverage patterns, and those elusive, missing pieces to draw meaningful comparisons and spotlight where the real story lies

5.3 Project Presentation: Conclusions, recommendations and next steps

    a. Drawing the line between independent investigators and the dependent actors we investigate

    b. Presenting clear and useful follow-up actions to clients and stakeholders without falling into decision-making traps

5.4 Post Investigation: Information-coping skills for self-managing our digital interactions

    a. Keeping the right doors open for continual discovery and professional growth

    b. Applying research disciplines to routines for managing our personal brands, virtual identities, and offline realities

Unit Five Benefits

- Differentiate deliberate from serendipitous discoveries
- Pinpoint conflicts of interest among our search targets
- Know where the bones are buried *before* you dig them up
- Legitimize the correct claims about conflicting facts and numbers
- Know and document the difference between confirmable facts and educated guesses
- Map research to primary intelligence and opportunities to barter information
- Assess the attention paid to our search topic and/or target and the broader issues they address

Unit Five Tables

- The certainty continuum for assessing the black and white (and gray)
- The candor of strangers and the corrupting influence of friendship
- The compromises to sound judgment posed by instant information
- Conversational icebreakers for breaking the case wide open
- Discussion maps for connecting the interests of our search targets to our project goals

UNIT SIX:
The Knowledge-ABLED Cook Book
Using Information:
A Recipe for Success

UNIT SIX SUMMARY

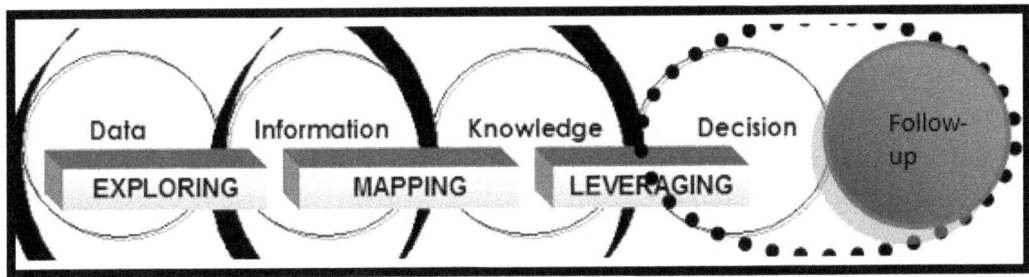

The book concludes with a Knowledge-ABLED use case based on the professional transformation of a commercial video producer to an educational media consultant. This use case guides us through the false starts and initial frustrations to the firmer footing and ultimate confidence-building that comes with being knowledge-ENABLED.

All relevant practices, frameworks, and search strategies in the case study are referenced to the specific units and chapters where they're introduced and demonstrated. For instance our use case subject entrepreneur plots out his research goals and supporting tasks through the Search Project Management model.

He applies the principles of site selection and Oceans, Lakes and Ponds to determine his sources, generate business leads, and build his understanding of the market and its growth potential. Finally he uses provider conjugation as a way of engaging the very same business contacts that first landed on his radar as search targets.

This journey is mapped out in three sections:

1. **The Diagnosis** – We find out what makes our entrepreneur tick, how he's transitioning careers, and his challenges both as a researcher and a marketer.

2. **The Search** – We apply the models and methods introduced in the first five units of the book to help scale the virtual research walls that were blocking the entrepreneur in the first section of **Unit Six**.

3. **The Engagement** – We see the pay offs from the results of Part Two through our subject's ability to generate business leads, develop networking contacts, and narrow down to a selective and promising market niche.

Unit Six Section Structure

6.1 Introduction: Food for thought: you are what you eat

    a. Defining culinary metaphors and applying them to the research process, such as...

    b. Main ingredients, meal types, cuisines, courses and cooking methods

6.2 The Diagnosis: Assessing the goals and challenges of our case subject

    a. Initial intake – Coming to terms with internet confusion

    b. Better business targeting through site selection – Building credibility through reporting requirements

    c. Defining the boundaries – Scoping out the SPM to keep the project online and in line with our objectives

6.3 The Search: Matching the pursuit to the pay-offs

    a. The information ocean for generating and qualifying business leads

    b. The information lake for assessing market studies

    c. The information pond to get from trapping to acting on what we learn

    d. The book on RSS feed readers and their functions and benefits

6.4 The Engagement: The transition from searching to conversing

    a. Listening to markets – How to use RSS as a survey tool for mapping and confirming trends

    b. A review of the site selection techniques used to uncover the sources used in the case study

    c. The provider conjugation method for assessing the motives of information suppliers and how our subject is viewed by others as an information provider in his own right

Unit Six Benefits

- Use term expansion to segment markets
- Understand the situational specifics and efficiencies in the local search, clipping, and alerting functions of RSS readers
- Connect individual experts to their key affiliations and then learn which groups are worth approaching
- Generate feeds from news queries, news sites, and social media sources (event triggers)
- Design a proactive follow-up to business leads triggered by daily events

Searching Out Loud: Curriculum Guide and Book Structure | c:17

Unit Six Tables

- Assembling the meal
- Gathering the research
- Mapping OLP to actions and outcomes
- Search Project Management Plan for our use case, (a.k.a. "George Reis Productions")

While not part of the curriculum guide, **Unit Seven** *lays out next steps for applying the perennial lessons of Searching Out Loud in the changing dynamics between information providers and tomorrow's Knowledge-ABLED investigators.*

UNIT FOUR:
SENSE-MAKING THROUGH INFORMATION CONTEXT

Taken into Context

In the previous unit we began to look at search results in terms of quality and quantity. We also learned how to assess information suppliers through **Source Fluency** and **Quality Control**. These methods are designed to improve the quality of the information we source from the web.

However, if we rely on sourcing alone we're still missing an essential ingredient in the search mix. That's the critical question of social information or context– how all this quality information is perceived by others:

- Who's aware of it?
- How does it help or hinder one's own objectives?
- Where do our findings deviate from the awareness baseline: What a layperson would learn about the same search target (without the tools and methods we're tapping into here?)
- When are we likelier to be believed or seriously questioned by those impacted by our research?

It's no longer the information supply but the demand side of web content be we'll consider in **Unit Four**. Context is what we still need to address before we produce our reports and lock-in our recommendations. Context must be established before we can meet our clients and colleagues with full confidence in our findings and accounting for our conclusions.

STUMBLING INTO CONTEXT

It's a paradox that the term 'context' is most commonly mentioned when it is missing from the discourse or situation in question. No one is said to *discover* context. The implicit understanding of context is that it lies there for the taking — like the numbers on a mailbox.

How often have we heard that the words of public figures and officials have been taken *out of context?* Now compare that with the number of times where a political rival, reporter, or intermediary was said to have taken the quoted source in the proper context? It's no contest.

Misunderstandings attract attention. Agreements are implied. So we take them for granted. There's no need to report them. In fact, it's because proper contexts go unreported that we need to understand them better as investigators. We are not involved in these discussions and the implicit assumptions they inspire. Investigators by our very nature are outsiders. We're more active as observants. Our capacities as team players are tested by the groupthink that develops when a band of like-minded insiders skirt the law. The insider sidesteps or suppresses conflicts-of-interest that place their own gain ahead of the larger groups or social forces they served, typically in a leadership context.

We will address context in a number of ways in **Unit Four**. We'll begin by examining the credibility of a website and the motivation of the information provider. Later, we'll learn how to evaluate the information exchange of others over the Internet. Finally, we'll turn our attention to a growing and prevalent form of group-think: The proliferation of social networks residing on the web. From a demand perspective, our interest is not about how to market one's services to friends or connections through a social site. It's how to deftly observe and assess the behaviors and tendencies of search targets as members of these communities.

Unit Four Learning Objectives

Let's take a glance back at the foundational settings from **Unit Three** that we'll be using as building blocks in **Unit Four**:

1. We established a set of quality controls to: (1) qualify, and (2) quantify the information we're sourcing from the initial search results, down to the site and page level of our sources.

2. We introduced source fluency as a way to attract quality information suppliers, even when targeting unfamiliar people and topics.

3. We considered how premium (or fee-based) information offers advantages to power users, a.k.a. investigators, insisting on the news origination and chronological sequencing often lacking in free public web sources.

4. We also addressed the 'Internet Radar' as a model for assessing the likely boundary lines between public and proprietary information – another key determinant in whether to opt for free or fee-based web content.

Unit Four builds on these foundations by focusing on the demand side of web content or the social dimension of digital information through...

- Group-based information – conflicts between personal loyalties, public credibility, and the need for group discipline
- Individual-based information – incentives to share and the inclination for belief through candor and authenticity
- Social networks and their impacts on both individuals and groups from the researchers' perspective

By mastering these skills, we will take our investigations to a deeper, more exhaustive level. We will look at the goals and motives of our search targets as both content producers and consumers. We will also see how these behaviors shift when we're investigating the same individual as a group member. What issues are addressed? Which ones are overlooked? We trace this back to the sincerity and goal orientation of individual versus group information providers.

Unit Four Destination: Evidence-gathering and Perspective-taking

Context is the one dimension from which information cannot be divided or filtered. By definition, context is the cross-referencing of two or more factors from which it forms. Maybe it's senders and receivers. Perhaps it's time and place. Remember all the dimensions we considered in compiling information types? Additional inputs like entry point, point of view, resources, and format all create the richer complexities that define the context. Context often does and should not exist in isolation, no matter how vehemently our accusers say we take them out of context.

UNIT FOUR: Sense-making Through Information Context | Page 4:3

In **Unit Four,** we will begin to apply situation appropriate tools and techniques to both traditional group-based and emerging individual-based information suppliers. We will be documenting the context, not only the content of the evidence we're citing. This requires that we create a framework for analyzing our search projects prior to presenting them in **Unit Five**. We will achieve this from the following perspectives:

1. **Persons of interest** – This is where our focus naturally shifts in criminal investigations, but also in business dealings where we're looking for contacts to influence or approve us and our clients as vendors

2. **Layperson** – The baseline for establishing awareness levels and common knowledge around the issues relevant to our project

3. **Third-parties** – Experts and experienced professionals with deep domain knowledge who have no vested interest in the outcome of our research efforts

Being able to process these frames of reference is the last critical piece between searching (query formation), sourcing (fluency), and delivery (final reporting). The perspective-taking framework aids our investigation in the following ways:

1. Enhances the perspectives of these other participants, without threatening the trust needed to embrace their full participation.

2. Explains the probable chain of events where scant documentation exists.

3. Analyzes the gap between words and deeds that explains the hypocritical behaviors we so often see between how we act as individuals and as group members.

4. Rationalizes the difference between public statements contained in sources like press releases, official records and policies versus personal disclosures that often run in conflict with on-the-record and contractual roles and responsibilities.

Definition: Context

The immediate circumstances that connect a single event to the broader meaning of motivations and perspectives of the actors in question.

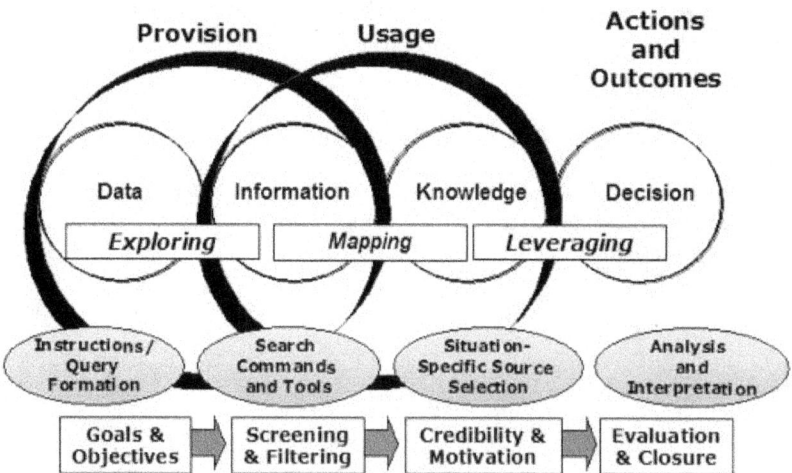

Along the Knowledge Continuum, we are now evaluating the credibility and determine the motivation that lies behind the information.

The demand side of the Knowledge Continuum is where we anticipate actions and outcomes. It's also where we conduct perspective-taking on what others will think or do once made aware of the information we gather – even the reports we're piecing together.

Unit Four bridges the 'what' to 'when' steps of the SPM process. That means that we're transitioning now from what are expectations are to when we'll pursue both missing and disputed details firsthand. In terms of sources and search results, what are some educated guesses about what we'll discover? In terms of *when,* that means when we'll engage our search targets directly – either virtually or in-person.

Our device for doing so is through the prismatic lens of provider conjugation. Provider conjugation builds on the source fluency methods we learned in the last unit by describing the context of the information we're evidencing as researchers. There are three basic ways we will come to define, view, interpret, and apply this framework to the analytical requirements of our investigations:

1. **Individual-based information** – incentives to share and the inclination for belief through candor and authenticity
2. **Group-based information** – conflicts between personal loyalties, public credibility, and the need for group discipline
3. **Social networks** – their impacts on both individuals and groups, from the researchers' perspective

Unit Four Benefits

Unit Four shows participants how to proceed from the collection to the analytical phase of their search projects. This is the sense-making stage that all investigations reach between the discovery process and delivering those findings, often with a set of recommendations and/or a plan for actions.

Upon completion of this unit, you should be able to find not only the facts and opinions we addressed in the last unit but the context of *how* and even *why* this evidence was reported. Here are those learning objectives we will master based on the three main sections within **Unit Four**:

Individual-based Information

- Recognize information providers' perspectives from the vantages of insiders and outsiders
- Distinguish between perceptions of private (informal) and public (formal) communications
- Recognize perception differences between firsthand and secondhand experiences and their impact on information providers and users
- Assess conflicts of interest, hidden agendas and predetermined limits on the range of encouraged or 'acceptable outcomes'

UNIT FOUR: Sense-making Through Information Context | Page 4:5

Group-based Information

- Recognize the institutional biases of third-hand information providers
- Group media sources by their business objectives and traditional cultural roles
- Recognize the ability of groupings of news media sources to shape public awareness and opinions around sensational crimes

Social Networks

- Assess and monitor the group behaviors and participation patterns formed in virtual communities
- Define the failsafes and terms of success on *people searches* and the grounds for closing such investigations
- Assess the differences between the way information is communicated informally through word-of-mouth and institutionally through groups

Search to Converse ("STC")

- When it makes sense to engage a search target directly and whether it's best to do that virtually or in-person
- Background research the people you're going to meet
  – Deploy specialized search tools to gauge their web presence and digital identities
- Build a stable of advisers and referral networks for finding experts and second opinions
- Pick a blogging theme that can used as a professional calling card (and showcase for our research)

Misinformation as an Information Source

- Apply the **Vectors of Integrity** to determine the credibility of information providers, and their own involvement in the issues they report
- Gauge the reputation of our search targets (it's not in the eye of the beholder!)

The Value of Social Information

- Test our knowledge through virtual networks
- Apply visualization tools to our networks
- Leverage social networking tools to raise our digital profile as an independent investigator
- Use alerts and notifications to stay on top of fluid and evolving situations

Searching Out Loud

SECTION 4:1 | Individual-based Information —
Personal Motivation

Why do people do what they do? Okay – for now that's above our pay grade. How about this: What are some common motives for sharing our views on social media pages, discussion boards, news articles, in blog postings, YouTube videos, etc.?

Common Forms of Motivation for Message Senders

- Justice
- Revenge
- Redemption
- Ego

Okay, so how well does the sending impulse sound to the ear of the recipients?

Common Forms of Motivation for Receivers

- Impartial
- Vested
- Action-based
- Comprehensive

It's funny. But when we look at the pay-offs, none of these emotional satisfactions include cash or material gain of any sort. It's also ironic that each one of these universally-held desires is in direct conflict with the other. A hard-nosed assessment is compromised by owning a direct stake in the outcome of that evaluation. A report predisposed to swift and certain actions is slowed down by the weight of due diligence and the need for broad-based input. The universal desire for an informed decision is not so easily satisfied. What seems reasonable as a single objective can become complicated or even at odds with other dual objectives:

1. How do we sort this out? How do we derive the context of our research findings?
2. Where does context meet up with our own conclusions and recommendations?
3. Do we show all our investigative cards? Do we hold them in reserve to appear less partial than we may be letting on?
4. Why is it essential that when we report our findings to clients and colleagues, that we also share a repeatable and simple model on which our assertions are based?

INTRODUCING PROVIDER CONJUGATION FRAMEWORKS

Provider conjugation is a lot like verb conjugation.

Remember when we took a foreign language in grammar school? We could always memorize the nouns. But we really couldn't speak in sentences until we learned how to conjugate the verbs. The same is true within the *to inform* aspect of information. *How* it travels from person-to-person and group-to-group is every bit as important to our understanding as the content of what's communicated.

Remember all those rhetorical battles pitting style against substance? The medium is the message and the power of the media? Conjugating providers is not only about communication styles. It's even more useful in trying to decipher what folks do with information once new information is added to one's existing knowledge and prior experience. It's not about a piece of information. It's about a piece of the action – the actions taken by ourselves and others when we're informed, and more to the point, *how* we are informed.

PCF is a model that combines the concept of individual and plural verb forms with the framework of degrees of separation. Taken together, source conjugation helps us to understand the distance between the information provider and their proximity to their information source. Are they one in the same? Did it happen to them directly – are they the news provider and news source? How does this both strengthen and compromise authority figures fond of quoting themselves, in the first person, in the third?

What if they're the intermediary? Say the reporter who receives the confession that solves the mystery? Does she go behind the perpetrator's back and spill the beans to the authorities? Was it an affront to the perpetrator? Is he part of a network where another members comes forward with information now relevant to a related and open investigation?

> *Definition: Provider Conjugation Frameworks ("PCFs")*
>
> *A model that determines the degree of separation between information sources (or messages) and information providers (messengers). PCFs are also used to clarify what information recipients do with information once it becomes assimilated into existing knowledge and prior experience.*

Transparency

Who-knew-what-and-when-did-they-know-it is a phrase made famous in the Watergate investigation of the early 1970s. Journalists have their inverted pyramids and attorneys have this familiar concept for framing the details of a public investigation. However, we can't fill-in the *who* and *when* particulars until we factor in transparency or the third-person element in source conjugation.

The notion of who knew what and when is not just about information sources and providers. If it was, there would be no calls for investigation. In an truly open source world, all cases would be closed.

Successful investigations rest on two bedrock notions:

1. Persons of good faith will come forward to steer the investigator in the right direction.

2. Criminal evidence lives on in the heads of those they confide in, no matter how careful the masterminds are in burying that body of knowledge.

There could be nothing written down, no recordings of any spoken evidence. Just winks, nods, and a feint grimace or facial tic. But a body of evidence is truly unrecoverable if there is no third-person. This is an observer, not an accomplice. The third-person is not directly involved in the planning, execution, or potential consequences of the plot in question. Looking for your person of good faith to come forward? Don't look in the first or second person of your source conjugations.

The Giant Listening Ear

Transparency is not limited to individuals. It's an important aspect in the source conjugation of groups too. Group communications by definition are not two-way but three way transactions that include first, second, and third parties: The message maker, provider, and its receivers.

How we're informed as members of groups is typically a more passive act than how we interact as individuals. That's because when we communicate in groups, we are either seeking an audience or forming one. It's even easier if the group has already assembled at a pre-arranged time. We attend the meeting in listen mode. We buy a ticket and find our seat. We flip on a switch. Presto! We're receiving the same signals as every audience member. And the communication is traveling our way in two forms: (1) the substance of the message itself, and (2) the social context shared by the message receivers.

This premise rests on the following inferences:

- How big our message receiving group is
- The common bonds, shared priorities, and rallying points that unify us
- Other events, people, and outcomes the group references in its reactions
- What kind of commitment the message sender seeks from us (our rapt attention for starters!)

Transparency in group communications is not limited to big media events. Sometimes the third wheel in a two-way dialog is not tuning into a regularly scheduled program or an updated web page. Sometimes that giant listening ear is not sitting in the studio audience but crouched in a van with headphones and a device for taping discussions they are privy to, but not present in.

For example, in a sting operation there are investigators that overhear evidence through wiretaps and eavesdropping. We are horrified when we as third-parties learn that an elected official is trying to trade public appointments for personal privilege. We're not aghast at the politician's hypocrisy but that his indiscretion was done with the knowledge he was under investigation – again the third leg of a two way communication.

Three Way Conversation

In fact, all public discourse is a three-way. When the celebrated TV interviewer interviews TV celebrities, it is the audience that creates the social value communicated by the newsmaker and intermediary. No matter how intimate the settings or revealing the subject, the prying eyes of the camera form a peep hole for the viewer. It may be fiction. It may be a fabrication. Either way, this a social exchange witnessed by countless people with no personal connection to either party. The role of celebrity enables us to relate to these otherwise strangers as members of groups – not directly as individual acquaintances but indirectly as observers, as fans, as audience members, as site visitors.

The more direct the connection between provider and subject, the greater the information provider's authenticity. *We believe that they believe what they believe.* Their authenticity is often conveyed in a stage whisper style. Authentic leaders can rally large crowds while commanding the intimacy of a much smaller group setting.

Authentic speakers introduce higher probabilities of tampering and distortion — especially when the provider's belief lies in their ability to influence, not in the actual facts selected or supporting details, if they're even offered. Unsupported evidence requires the close loyalties of recipients who pledge a faith-based allegiance to a higher truth, transcending the empirical inspection of facts on the ground.

I've never been a fan of three ways. Two way conversations are tough enough for me to keep track of. To be frank, sometimes talking privately with one's self can feel like a noisy and crowded room. Crack a window. It's stuffy in there!

The Three Tenses

Returning to our conjugation model, we remember that there are three types of conjugation:

I, you, and they, or first, second, and third person.

In PCF, this denotes the singular form for individuals and plural for groups. We express this as first, second, and third *person* for individuals. We refer to first, second, and third *parties* for groups. The source conjugation framework provides us perspective in (1) connecting information sources to their suppliers, and (2) how these providers behave as soloists and in groups.

Let's contrast persons and parties. First we'll map two opposing vectors which we'll chart more fully later in this section. We will connect *credibility* to third party information sources and *authenticity* to first person participation – someone on the *front lines* of public conflict (soldiers, medics, firefighters, law enforcement, campaign workers, etc.)

Who are the go-betweens? Who are the intermediaries between the first and third tenses? Those would be second person informants and confidantes. Second parties are not only recipients but sources in their own right for passing on their own assessments onto third parties. Think of the traditional relationship of newspaper reporters to readers, and expert witnesses to jurors. Second parties are always one step removed from the actions they assess and the potential outcomes they may trigger.

Ultimately, PCF ("Provider Conjugation Framework") is designed to help the Knowledge-ABLED on two fronts...

1. **As researchers:** Understand the motivations of senders and receivers, and

2. **As investigators:** Engage experts and decision-makers within our passionate interests, fields of choice, and chosen communities.

How Information Travels

In addition to senders and receivers, we need to deepen the conjugal model by laying the groundwork for the transfer: How is this information transferred or exchanged? Applying PCF to context triggers questions about the nature of the exchange:

1. Are we communicating with one or many?

2. Is it the intimacy of one trusted adviser?

3. Is it an announcement that we've crafted to hundreds of former colleagues that we've accepted an offer with a new employer?

4. Is it somewhere in the middle where we're reaching out to groups and selective members?

THE THREE TYPE OF INFORMATION EXCHANGES

In addition to the three PCF tenses, it is also important to factor in the nature of how providers choose to communicate. These are the kinds of information exchange that describes the relationship between senders and receivers. There are three information exchanges:

1. Source to listener (1:1) – first person/party (one-on-ones are both intimate and unstructured)

2. Source to small group (1:several) – second person/party

3. Source to large group (1:many) – third person/party

Who Belongs Where?

The source conjugation chart below defines individual and group information exchanges according to the role of the information giver. These examples parallel the information sources and recipients that are common to criminal investigations:

FIGURE 4.1: Provider Conjugation Framework ("PCF") for Assessing Personal Motives

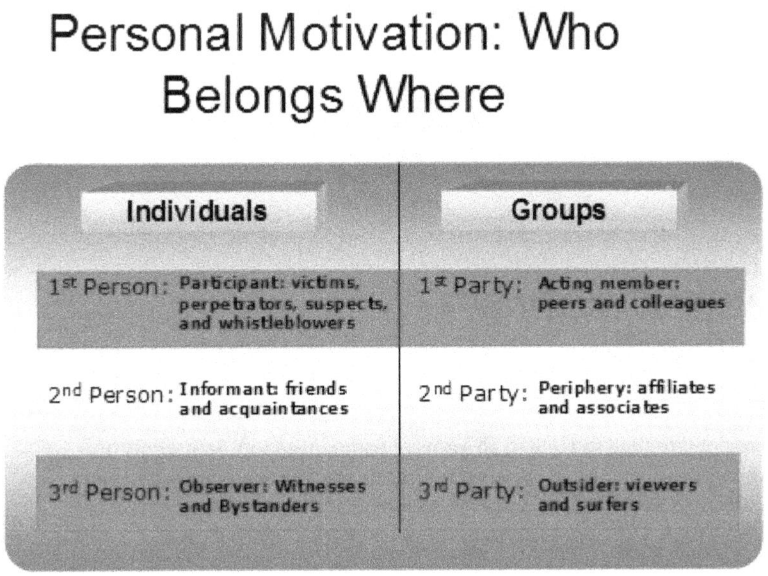

Personal Motivation: Who Belongs Where

Individuals	Groups
1st Person: Participant: victims, perpetrators, suspects, and whistleblowers	1st Party: Acting member: peers and colleagues
2nd Person: Informant: friends and acquaintances	2nd Party: Periphery: affiliates and associates
3rd Person: Observer: Witnesses and Bystanders	3rd Party: Outsider: viewers and surfers

In the diagram above we're seeing two levels emerge here: 1. Individuals – represent personal opinions and individual choices. This is the province of private matters, informal exchanges, and casual conversation. 2. Groups – represent group consensus, dissent and affiliation (label, brand, party affiliation, etc.)

Who Belongs Where – Applying the Framework

PCFs are perspective-gathering tools for understanding the context of information exchanges. Instead of focusing on the message, we look at the roles we're used to performing ourselves – or seeking out in others:

1. How would we use this framework to plot the roles and motivations of our search targets?
2. Where are there natural connections between informants and investigators? Where are there natural blockages?
3. What alternatives are available to the resourceful investigators?
4. How do the roles change from personal involvement at an individual level to playing a professional role at the group level?

FIGURE 4.2: PCF for Ascribing Roles and Responsibilities

	Individuals		Groups
1st Person:	Primary source: diaries and interviews	1st Party:	Vested authority: speeches and roundtables
2nd Person:	Voucher: cross-checking and verifications	2nd Party:	Reporter: articles and investigations
3rd Person:	Commentator: interpretation and conjecture	3rd Party:	Researcher: surveys and forecasts

CONTAINERS OF INFORMATION EXCHANGES WITHIN GROUPS

"I know more than I can say. I say more than I can write down."

– David Snowden, Founder, Cognitive Edge

These exchanges that we are placing within the PCF are not intended to scale to all forms of communication. Transcripts of most therapy sessions don't get uploaded to mytherapysessions.com. Most lawyer-client communications are privileged and are implicitly off limits to investigators, if they are documented at all. That said, we are including a broader representation of interactions than what will turn up in a web-based investigation. Our purpose is to make sense of the many digitized messages that lack context or a basis for...

- Assessing the motivations of senders, or
- How receivers process, frame, and potentially act on them.

Anyone who ever studied a second language in grammar school can recall how traditional conjugation methods address informal and formal second person verb tenses. In provider conjugation, this distinction is expressed as:

1. Internal (informal or casual) communication, and
2. External (formal or official) communication

Figure 4.3 shows the conduits or media for hosting and conveying these exchanges within two types of groups:

1. **Internal Groups:** Communities of personal contacts – This kind of communication is generally expressed through word-of-mouth or informally communicated through face-to-face communications. Not surprisingly, the explosive use of social media has redefined the boundaries of internal communities within a largely open, virtual setting.

2. **External Groups:** Communities of impersonal contacts – This kind of communication is conveyed through public forums or *the media* and is usually more formally stated. It is implicitly group-based and generally passes through multiple stakeholders before it is released to a wider audience of second and third parties.

FIGURE 4.3: Internal and External Communications

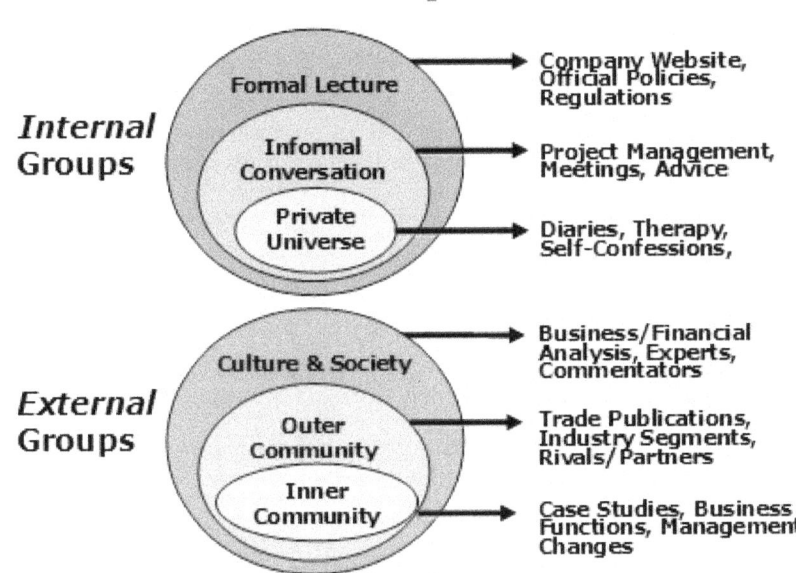

The Intermingling of Persons and Parties

Does that mean singular and plural are isolated from one another? Not in the slightest. Not only do individuals address groups. Groups dress down individuals. In delicate matters, we are prone to intimate exchanges with members of external groups. We look to trained counselors and professionals such as doctors, attorneys, and therapists. In those cases we may be preparing for a difficult conversation with a loved one or girding for a legal battle. Whatever the confrontation that lies ahead, our instincts for validation and detached feedback are often served by seeking advice. That trusted advisor belongs to a disinterested second party, not through the direct involvement of a vested second person.

Second Parties as Communication Vessels

Second parties often act as conduits between first and third parties. An office colleague could function as a second party. So can advisers like job coaches, stockbrokers, or the clergy. All require an additional layer of second party detachment in order to provide community leadership and the professional perspective and personal bond required in these roles. Third parties are creatures of the aggregate. That means large groupings of people who share an ordinary and passive bond as consumers (shoppers, demographics, fan clubs), and citizens (voters, taxpayers, volunteers, etc.)

Provider Conjugation: Individual and Group Motivation Vectors

The most accomplished web investigator never forgets how hard it is to truly nail a question that has many angles, nuances and shadings. But if we break our problems down to the PCF model, it's easier to see where the personal element figures into real world events, opportunities, and outcomes. We are several steps ahead of the targets we're investigating if we can speak to the context of our evidence-gathering. We won't have produced a better answer with a team behind us and an open-ended project calendar if we don't place our questions in the correct context. Neither will we lose any perspective from severing our reliance on social media where the personal touch is diminished by our in-network connections or distorted by the conforming pressures of virtual group behaviors (public shaming, compromising memes, etc.).

The next section introduces vectors for describing the perspectives of information providers. This includes the full conjugal range of first and second persons and parties. What powers of persuasion do these message senders summon within the range of their experience? How do they get their points across? Each conjugal provider is set to a standard scale of information attributes. Each attribute can be expressed as a vector that maps the motivations present when information is imparted from providers to receivers.

This helps us understand their incentives for making their messages known to us whether the carrier is an email, a blog post, a Facebook wall, a press release, or a journal entry. Motivation vectors of information exchange can also help us evaluate the nature of both individual and group exchanges.

Our analysis of these vectors includes the following dimensions:

- **Perspective** – Is this work self-referential or grounded in a more group-based agenda?
- **Documentation** – What is the likelihood these details have been (1) recorded, and (2) made accessible to us?
- **Verbiage** – What kinds of word choices (or semantics as we discussed in **Unit Two**) are unique to the situational specifics of the evidence in question?
- **Medium** – What is the transmission method likeliest to have distributed the evidence in question (book, database, web page, listserv, text message, public venue, etc.)

Individual: First Person

All messages begin to some extent in the mind of the individual before they're ever typed, edited, published, or disputed. There are no intermediaries or interpreters or critiques. All paths lead from first person whether or not that individual chooses to document and share their ideas. What form does this take? What's the incentive to do so? What does first person even sound or look like? The motivation vectors help guide our thinking here about the self-referential nature of first-person exchanges.

- **Perspective** (motive of information provider): "I am therefore I exist"
- **Documentation** (form of documentation): Last Wills and Testaments
- **Verbiage** (economy of detail): Prayers
- **Medium** (form of delivery): Safety deposit box; personal journal; voice-over
- **Temptation** (exclusive property or privilege of provider): Relationship status on Facebook

FIGURE 4.4: First Person Motivation Vector

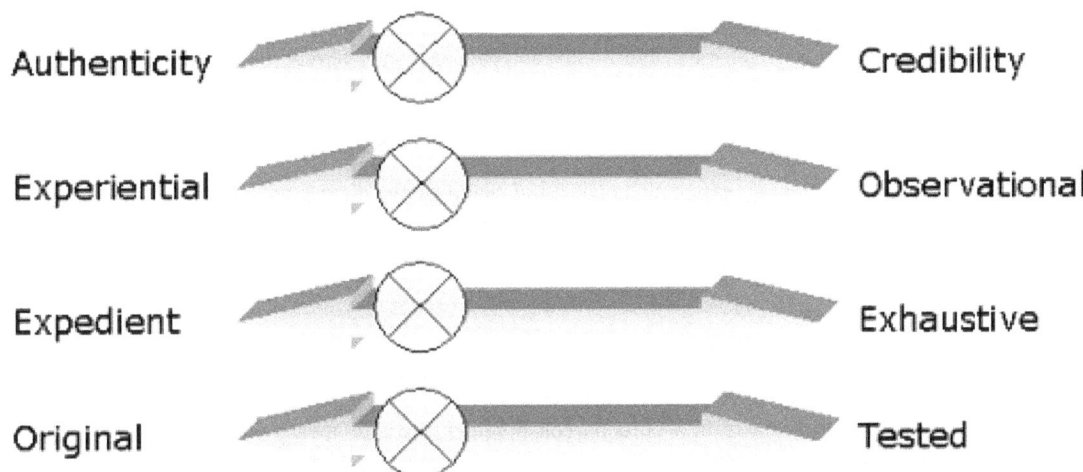

Vector two can apply to a writers' perspective. This means that all first person narratives are by definition the direct experience of the author when chronicling one's own accounts and viewpoints.

<u>Vector Ranges</u>

There is no audience so there is no need to persuade with the head or conceal from the heart. First person is the center of abject authenticity. There's no pretending or protecting or points to negotiate. The heart believes what it believes beyond any reasonable doubt. There are no justifications for its actions or the laws and policies that frame our professional conduct and organizational behavior. This is the gut talking and it is uninhibited by prying ears, competing explanations, and the hindsight used to rationalize the instinctive nature of its most intimate details.

First person accounts tend to run from due process and lose patience with the complexities that turn black and white situations into gray. First person narratives doesn't wait around to hear the other side of stories already concluded – hence the expedient nature of first person. Ironically, this is both the most compelling evidence for answering why people commit unspeakable acts in their own incriminating words.

<u>Discussion Points</u>

- Where are the blindspots of first person accounts on the web? How can we use source fluency to reduce them or be receptive to learning from them by sources we would otherwise spurn or ignore?
- Where would our information sources in our current investigations fall in the spectrum?
- Do they assume a personal or professional role and how does this potentially serve as well as compromise our own objectives in the case?

Individual: Second Person

There is a second person reckoning once a first-person message is intercepted by a receiver. Sometimes this is a passive role as a listener or a lurker. Sometimes a more active voice can mean interpreting and passing alone a filtered version of a first person story to the larger group. Sometimes the second person is not a go-between but a resource, responding directly to the comments and questions posed by the first person. From an Internet perspective, think of this interaction as an informal collaboration between individuals with a mutual concern and the direct experience they draw from to express this.

Layperson medical communities are a prime example. It's easier to compile list of well-regarded disease-related social networks based on firsthand referrals than to reach consensus about the websites best equipped to address which treatments to consider for the same illness. That's because second person trumps third party both in terms of sincerity and familiarity. Victims and their families telling their stories, trading advice, and coping with their afflictions by sharing first-hand experience through electronic word-of-mouth.

Vector Ranges

One way to look at second person discussions is whether we're prefer an open social media environment or a closed loop like email. The former is easier to capture, archive, and attracts more potential collaborators. The latter means we have a much clearer idea of who we're communicating with. In opting for email this choice is expressed well by a local colleague of mine named Sadie Van Buren who writes:

> *"I'm not so much looking to leverage the experience of people I don't know as desiring to make a connection with those I do."*

As researcher/observers in these forums we need to consider the chumminess factor. Are first and second persons offline friends and colleagues or are they strangers who meet virtually over a common interest? This vector shows how to interpret the notable differences between first- and second-person information exchanges.

- **Perspective:** "We're on the same page"; crowdsourcing
- **Documentation:** Memorandums; testimonial
- **Verbiage:** Communities of practice; conference call
- **Medium:** Email; group discussion boards
- **Temptation:** Spilling a secret a first person has sworn to their safekeeping

FIGURE 4.5: Second Person Motivation Vector

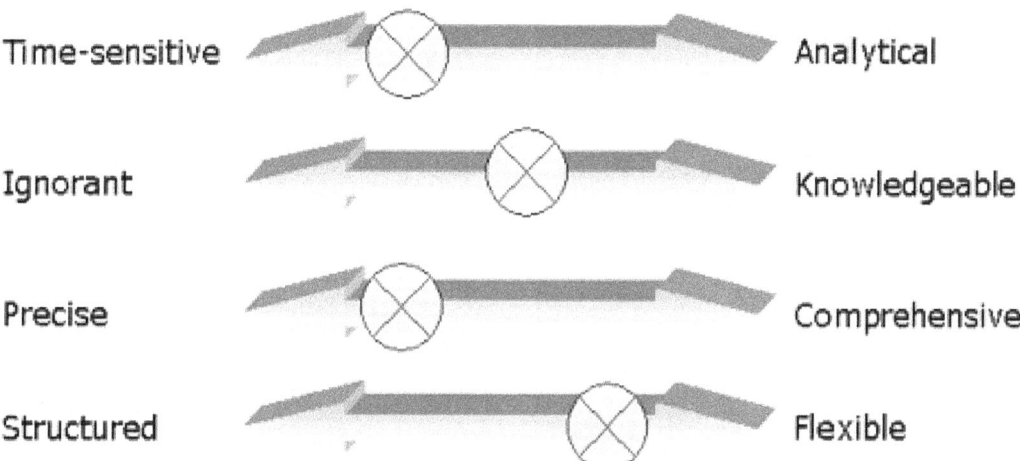

Second person, like first person, is fluid, freewheeling, and for the most part unfiltered. A sender's awareness of a confidante or small group of receivers will prompt self-censoring, particularly if they are seeking counsel.

<u>Discussion Points</u>

- In vector 2, first person knowledge seekers meet up with second person responders. Is the second person better equipped to offer comfort or expertise? That's a key consideration when determining whether such feedback may be used for coercive or educational purposes – think political lobbying.

- Vector 3 might be a status check or a debrief such as the exit interview given by a departing employee. A fifth vector might be presentational or formal communications versus conversational or more informal exchanges.

- What doubts and uncertainties can we expect in word-of-mouth exchanges? How do we apply PCF to meetings where two parties start on the same page and leave the same meeting with diverging or even clashing interpretations?

- If word-of-mouth is such a flexible medium, what does that say about the documentation (or accountability) of these exchanges? How well does social media capture the dynamic of a roundtable discussion? How about a call-in show between a regular listener and a panel of experts? The dynamic is beholden to the channel of that communication — just as much as the points raised by the caller or shared across our table of experts.

INDIVIDUAL: THIRD PERSON

Who's the third person? That would be us – assuming we don't know anyone we're investigating. The irony is that even if we do, we need to develop a third eye that sees the world from the lens of a third-person. This is someone who may take notice of the discussion but is disinterested in the first and second persons. They are not vested in any specific outcomes. They have no *skin in the game*. That makes them ideal for passing judgments because they can focus on the merits of an argument instead of the interpersonal dynamics that cloud the judgments of first and second persons. That's why this vector considers the elevated perspectives of detached observers.

That detachment includes a sensitivity towards sequence. In the case of first and second parties, that means identifying who speaks first and the dynamic it triggers. Does our first person continue to break the ice by introducing related topics and concerns? Does a second person steer the conversation in a completely new direction? The assertiveness of message senders and receivers is key to understanding their roles and influence in these exchanges. It's a dynamic less likely to escape the attention of a seasoned third person than someone directly involved in the discussion.

Vector Ranges

If third persons have a common bias, it's that they remain so. They prefer their independence to the commitment of active participation. We will see how this plays out in the insider and outsider roles assumed in the group behaviors of third parties. For now, we think of third parties as the clear-eyed stranger that we open up to on a long bus or flight, knowing that we will part company at the end of the trip in complete anonymity. It's the impersonal nature of third person affiliations that gives us the freedom to be astute judges of character, thorough researchers, and ultimately, effective investigators.

- **Perspective:** 'Rules and procedures'
- **Documentation:** Employee handbook; arbitration guidelines
- **Verbiage:** The passenger in the middle seat (we're on the aisle of the same row)
- **Medium:** 3-ring binder; jury box
- **Temptation:** Crawl under a rock until the crowd clears out

FIGURE 4.6: Third Person Motivation Vector

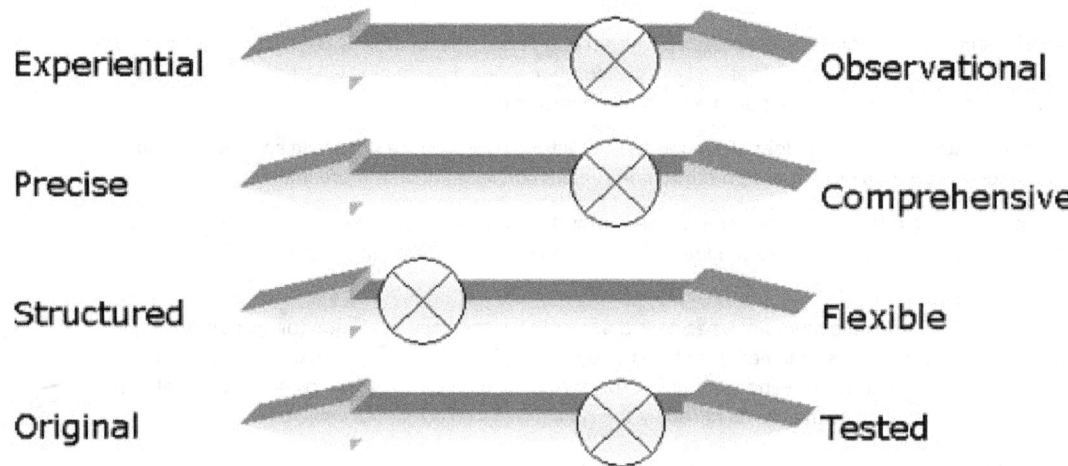

Third persons don't hang on the details of the first person's breathless accounts. Third persons may be drawn into conflicts at random as innocent bystanders. Their roles can also be more deliberate and clarifying when they function as the hypothetical 'every woman' or 'every man' meaning that they represent the approximated perception ranges of a grouping of people.

Discussion Points

- As vector 1 suggests, third persons insist on competing versions of the same story and can usually spot self-promotion and circular reasoning at the expense of a more balanced and evidence-based accounting.
- This skepticism suggests that vested opinions are vetted or tested against what the first or second person hopes to gain or influence in how and what they communicate to others.
- How does a third person perspective add to the endorsement or sanctioning of otherwise dubious ventures? How do we spot that an independent voice has been corrupted or co-opted by someone with a stake in the ground?
- What could it cost the information provider if such a credentialing backfired?

GROUP BEHAVIOR IN PROVIDER CONJUGATION

We all like to join groups. The most disagreeable curmudgeon takes solace and strength from being a card-waving member of the grumpy contrarian association. The reason we hear for this is that humans are 'social animals.' It's in our nature to bond with other tribal members. The less trumpeted reason is because being in a group can bring us power and influence that we could never wield as individuals.

As we just saw with individual conjugation, first persons have a tendency to pull third persons aside as control groups for confirming their own feelings and experiences. Then there's the validating power of third persons as proof these assertions are shared on a broader level. The punch line lands: "It's not just me!" That's a complex maneuver, no? It sounds like a variation on the Abbott and Costello baseball routine about 'who's on first?' ... 'I don't know who's on third!' ... and second base is not even on today's scorecard.

One of the great benefits to grouping individual behaviors is that it's easier to keep score. People band together because they all share the same priorities and viewpoints. There's no need to argue the point among members. This frees the group to make its case by marketing to individuals ("come join our crusade") or lobbying third parties:

> *"We are correct so vote for us,"*

> *"Rule in our favor,'*

> *"Change this law,"* etc.

The simplicity of uniform agreements held by all of its members does have a downside for groups. It buries dissension and discourages internal debate. It objectifies opposing points of view as not only different but inferior and lacking merit. This belief denies the other party the legitimacy and respect needed to come to accommodations that consider both sides. As satirist Jon Stewart points out, the other side is not simply the opposing side, but the *enemy.* There can be no other view but the one held by group members. The collective denial of a first party is the same as the self-deception of a first person – just on a wider scale

GROUP: FIRST PARTY

First parties are the collective form of self-interest. They are prone to overstepping their bounds when claiming to represent the interests of those falling outside the group. Political parties are prime examples, claiming that they are acting on behalf of much larger majorities than the actual numbers of the electorate that vote for their candidates.

The genesis of first parties is the universal human need to be part of something larger. Groups draw strength from a powerful desire to belong. Pressure to conform is almost irresistible – even when we're not members. Here's one example.

A hotel chain wants to save money on its cleaning operations so it hangs placards asking guests to reuse their towels to save energy and water. In the first attempt, the signs implore guests to join the crusade. Twelve percent go along. In the second attempt the hotel reasons that other guests are already doing this as a matter of habit. Over a third of the guests began doing so. The point here is that when made aware of them, we tend to stay in the boundaries of social norms – even when those definitions are designed to benefit the first parties who create them. Robert Ciardini calls it *social proof* – peer information, not peer pressure. **(Maney, 2009)**[1]

Vector Ranges

First parties are not all hellbent on conquering the world of public opinion or vanquishing the groups and policies that stand in their way. On a generic level, all organizational behavior falls under first party provider conjugation. There are protocols to follow whether we belong to an employer, a block association, or a mutual admiration society.

First parties are rife with conflicts of interest. First parties arouse suspicion whenever a mixed verdict is interpreted as a mandate to take actions that unites the party and supersedes the outcomes of any election. The larger the first party, the likelier that this is a domain where leaders and followers tend to congregate. A power structure emerges. Beliefs become systematized into codes. Representatives are elected to draft the rule-making that will be adopted by the larger body. Is this based on the consent of the members? What are the schisms that form around the rulings that follow? Is power-sharing part of the leadership role? How binding are these executive decisions? Does a void ensue between the rulers and the rank and file?

- **Perspective:** 'We lead – others follow'
- **Documentation:** Shredded
- **Verbiage:** Closed door meeting
- **Medium:** The White House lawn
- **Temptation:** Recruit outside analysts and experts for hire

FIGURE 4.7: First Party Motivation Vector

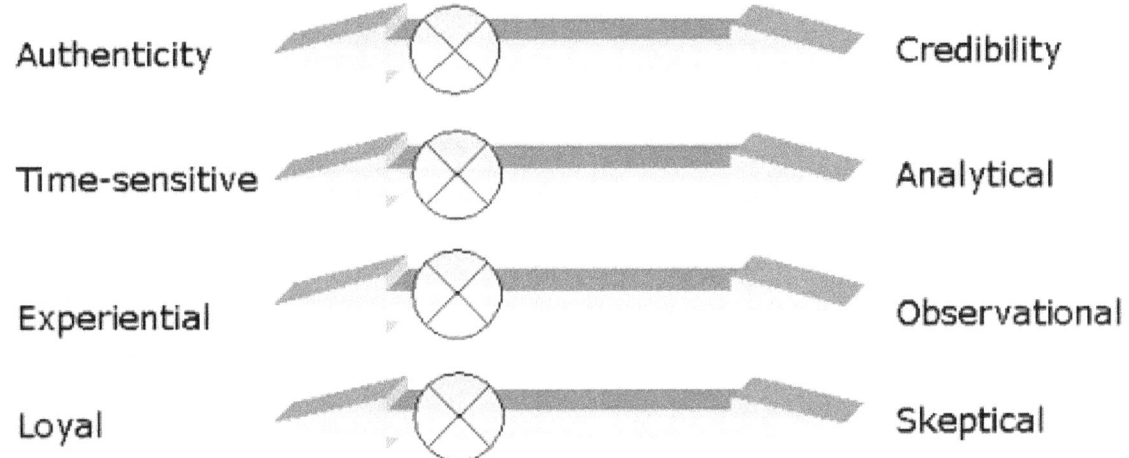

First parties share solidarity of belief that unifies them in their authenticity: (we believe that they believe what they communicate). This unity of the 'true believers' can also blind them to the views and beliefs of other groups as we see in vector 4.

FIGURE 4.8: Verbatim Query: First Persons Belong to Which First Party?

"we belong to a ****"

About 701,000 results (0.20 seconds)

We belong to a Yahoo group. When we read the messages with ...
Oct 19, 2010 ... A text box shows on the computer screen with the file name and the ... The owner of the group has two choices. One, the attachements can be ...
answers.yahoo.com/question/index?qid... - Cached

> Do you give your toddler a daily multivitamin? - Sep 27, 2010
> What hip-hop site do you belong to? - Aug 5, 2010
> More results from answers.yahoo.com »

Videos for "we belong to a ****"

Tim Neave - We Belong To A Time
51 sec - Feb 3, 2009
Uploaded by nunnytv
youtube.com

laura zimmerman manager of clintonville ...
7 min - Sep 27, 2010
vidds.net

Answers.com - Why do we belong to a diocese
Uncategorized question: Why do **we belong to a diocese?** Can you answer this question? ... Why do **we belong to a diocese?** In: Uncategorized [Edit categories] ...
wiki.answers.com/Q/Why_do_we_belong_to_a_diocese - Cached

Virginia Bed and Breakfast, Staunton, VA, Shenandoah Valley B&B ...
We belong to a local Farm Co-op, supplying us with fresh locally-grown organic produce from May through October. The Blackfriars' Playhouse, at The American ...
www.stauntonbedandbreakfast.com/ - Cached - Similar

Joe Cocker & Jennifer Warnes – Up Where We Belong – Video ...
Jun 11, 2010 ... Monday morning; karigasniemi added Up Where **We Belong to a deleted playlist. Monday** morning; phantomviper, skynet2777, skeetey and 8 other ...
www.last.fm/music/.../_/Up+Where+We+Belong - Cached - Similar

Environmental Commitment - bioMérieux Corporate Webportal site
"**We belong to a community**" is one of bioMérieux's guiding principles. At each of our sites and subsidiaries throughout the world, our employees are joining ...
www.biomerieux.com/servlet/srt/bio/portail/dynPage?... - Cached - Similar

Mutual Admiration Society (song) - Wikipedia, the free encyclopedia
[edit] The song. Ubiquitous in the mid to latter 1950s, the song is famous for its catchy chorus: **We belong to a Mutual Admiration Society,**: My baby and me. ...
en.wikipedia.org/wiki/Mutual_Admiration_Society_(song) - Cached - Similar

Discussion Points

- In Figure 4.7's vector 1, we see that authenticity overwhelms credibility. However, first parties like to co-opt credibility so that they are perceived as less self-serving by third person and third parties. This is a familiar pattern of corruption when the first party squelches potentially dissenting views or uses information providers from groups of their own creation to elevate their priorities and share their views.

- Where would we witness this conflict-of-interest? Typically, it's when we connect the first party's financing a stake in the third party that unduly praises or advocates their views. These are in fact second, and not third parties since their interests are now entwined with their sponsors.

- The authenticity of first parties is rooted in the direct experiential stake they place in their organizations and activities. When viewing them as outsiders, where would we look for fissures or cracks in party unity? How could that widen the gap between the group mission and the actual tactics it practices to achieve its aims?

- First party expediency and control enable swift decisions. In a crisis, first parties take precedence over the consensus building reached through second-party deliberation and validation. For example, leading armies into combat is first party communications premised on the practicalities of survival. As noted in vector 2, decisiveness is the only option.

- Most importantly what's the smell test for first party corruption? When the leader or a select group from within use their privileged status for their own advancement at the expense of the membership. That is the world's oldest profession in the hypocrisy business: *Watch not what I say but what I do...*

GROUP: SECOND PARTY

Second party sources consist of the professional community of business partners, shareholders, regulators, customers, and rivals who all have one stake in your organization's success and at least two stakes in their own.

We're all familiar with the sensation of being blindsided. Few of us have the presence of mind to see how our blindsides figure into this. Instead, we lash out at the tattle-tale (grammar school), newsleaker (media and politics) or smell a rat who disavowed a code of silence (organized crime and old boys networks). Either way, we aim to shoot the messenger when the message they bear has escaped into the open, too late to suppress. Whether the act is a heroic defiance or a backstabbing betrayal is in the eye of (1) those directly implicated in the disclosure (first parties), and (2) the folks who hear about it third-hand via the web (third parties). Either way, their judgments are cast in the direction of second parties.

UNIT FOUR: Sense-making Through Information Context | Page 4:23

Vector Ranges

In the first vector, it's ambiguous whether second parties are behaving in a conspiratorial or collusive way or whether they are acting in a credible manner. A fairly good indication is to consider the impact on the second party for making public their opinions, i.e. a local newspaper publishing the details of falling housing prices will potentially undercut its real estate classifieds – thus elevating its credibility.

In terms of perspective-taking, second party credibility is related to how much direct influence first parties wield on them. It is often more effective to go 'off record' with second parties to gain a more personal or authentic view than the official record provides.

Second parties lie at the root of two very prevalent and universal human sensitivities – envy and resentment. Envy is a factor in the minds of onlookers when peers raise their public profiles (and the privileges and rewards that bestows). The responsorial chant echoed in the fickle nature of public opinion is to dress down or dismiss the unworthy – those undeserving of third party recognition. Resentments are stirred not necessarily when second parties deliver the good news that happens to the unworthy. It's when bad news happens to us.

- **Perspective:** Who's ahead; who's losing ground
- **Documentation:** Gossip rag
- **Verbiage:** Speculation; rumor for its own sake
- **Medium:** Paparazzi; supermarket checkout line
- **Temptation:** Compensate the first parties they expose in their reporting and bill the third parties who subscribe to the information they supply

FIGURE 4.9: Second Party Motivation Vector

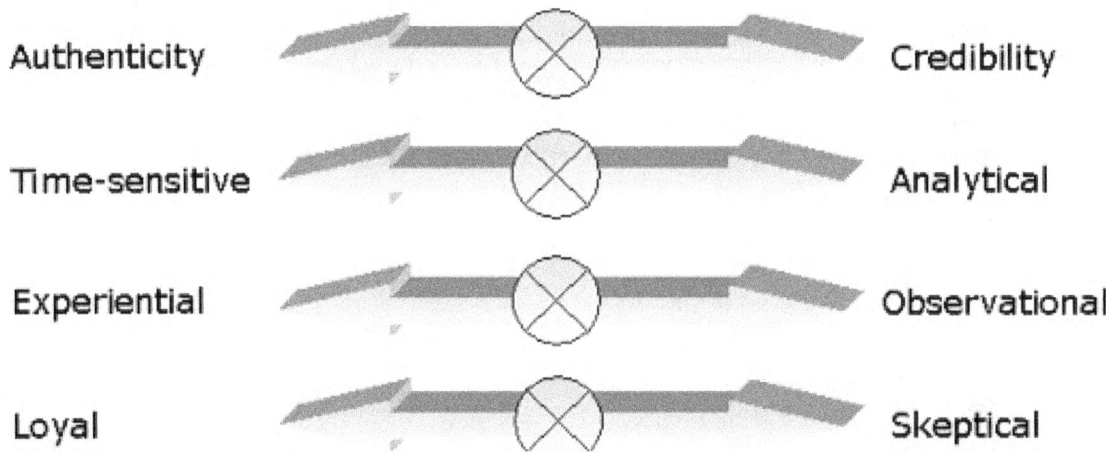

Second parties straddle the line between both ends of the motivation vectors. Too skeptical and they lose access to their first party networks. Too loyal and they may be tempted to protect their news sources from winding up as news. Too analytical and they miss their deadlines. Too authentic and their involvement supersedes the story they're covering.

UNIT FOUR: Sense-making Through Information Context | Page 4:24

FIGURE 4.10: Word Algebra Combined with Paradoxical Syntax: Talk about Mixed Signals!

Discussion Points

- How do second party dynamics play out? Try this out for size:

    The messenger communicates through the second party channel to the entire group, not directly to the person directly impacted, i.e. by a layoff or passed over for a promotion. Know the scene where the shunned party points first to the newspaper and then to the first party messenger? "It's bad enough you're making the wrong decision. But you had to go behind my back for me to find this out?" That's the comprising light of second party dynamics.

- How do second parties approach first parties? Do they tip their hands or expect the same intimacy or check-in privileges as the inner circle within the organizations they're approaching? Here's one noninvasive way to pry:

    By keeping our profiles low and egos in check, we can learn much about whether second parties are behaving in a conspiratorial or collusive way or whether they are acting in a credible manner. In terms of perspective-taking, second party credibility is related to how much direct influence first parties wield on them. A fairly good indication for us is gauging the impact on the second party for making public their opinions, i.e. a media organization admits on its own website to potential conflict-of-interest between its news coverage of companies who advertise on its site.

GROUP: THIRD PARTY

"The single biggest predictor of hostility is third person plural – defined by existence of the oppositional group."

– Pennabaker, Chung, 2007[2]

Third parties have several conjugal identities. The most common to the vernacular are acknowledged experts and analysts who are entrusted to put their subscribers' interests above those of the first parties they evaluate (see Figure 4.11 below). In our motivation vector model, third parties are on the receiving end of what's filtered or processed through first and second parties. Third parties are the audiences, the juries, the focus group panels, and the viewers furiously punching their votes into their devices. Broadly speaking, third party equals *the public*. The message is an *official* one once it reaches that level of circulation.

For that reason, off-the-record comments that would be tolerated or ignored among peers have the potential to become moral scandals once they reach third party level. Even the mechanics of message creation may be standard practice between colleagues. But in the wider public sphere, ghostwriting and the falsification of authorship is fair game for litigation. **(Elliot, 2010)[3]**

It's more complicated to reach the third party when a first party communicates through a second party. Why? They want to win more votes, sell more products, or simply to gain greater advantage with or without the participation of the larger society.

Third parties are the faces in the crowd who cast their votes, respond to surveys, and don't get hung up on their fifteen minutes of fame. Instead they have fifteen minutes per day that they use to read or hear about the fame of celebrities they follow. Third parties are the audience that assembles to hear speeches or consume the latest fashions. The media keep their finger on the pulse of third parties to determine social trends and cultural dimensions of what's falling in and out of favor.

Vector Ranges

Third parties as commentators and analysts speak in the media on behalf of abstractions like *the market,* or *the consumer,* or a disenfranchised group playing the role of underdog in a public debate. Third parties are also a common way for understanding exposure: Both positive, as in receiving popular recognition for a deed or achievement, and negative, where a person's reputation can be irrevocably damaged.

Those swings of the exposure pendulum are based on this other identity of third parties as *them*. The more removed, the more impersonal, the less vested, and detached from the actual consequences to individuals.

One way to distinguish this split identity for third parties is to think of third party experts as favoring complexity because complications require their direct input. The opposite holds true for third party audiences who are predisposed to simplicity and clear-cut distinctions.

How so?

Think of the superficial stereotypes that fill the void of real experience, i.e. pro-border Americans who think that legal and illegal immigrants can be easily separated.

- **Perspective:** Why should you care
- **Documentation:** Wall Street Journal; New York Times, etc. (exception is op-ed)
- **Verbiage:** Pundits analyze relevance of day's events
- **Medium:** Top news stories; most emailed stories
- **Temptation:** Have surrogates and representatives fight on their behalf without the need for direct involvement

FIGURE 4.11: Third Party Motivation Vector

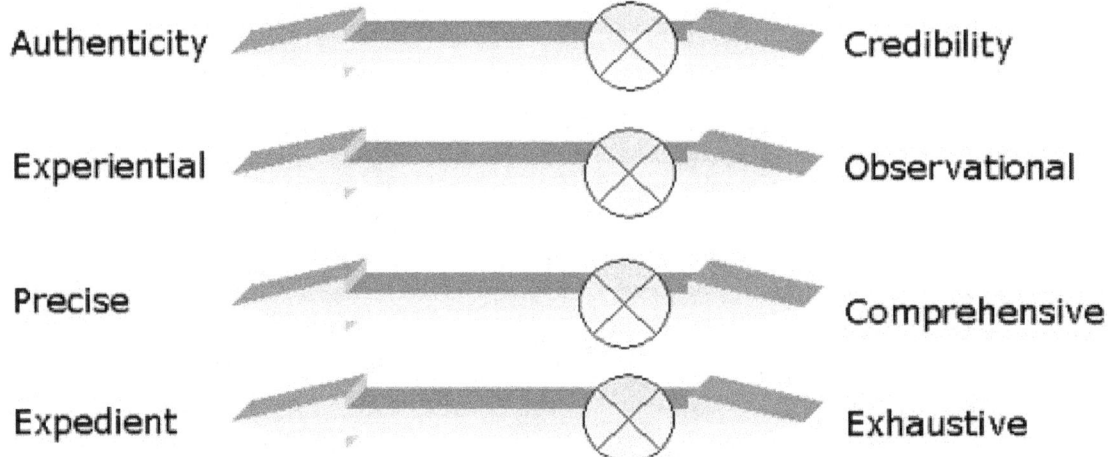

Third parties are two steps removed from the action. Third parties have the luxury of *taking in* or *thinking through* the issues of the day from the heated rhetoric and vested opinions of conflicting views and opposing camps.

FIGURE 4.12: Word Algebra Highlights the Possessive Attachment of These Detached Third Parties

"(analysts | researchers) * cover" ~compromise ~credible intitle:financial

About 152,000 results (0.37 seconds)

[PDF] The Rodney L. White Center for **Financial** Research Analyst ...
File Format: PDF/Adobe Acrobat - Quick View
by L Fang - 2004 - Cited by 10 - Related articles
compromised when the pressure for generating underwriting revenue, ... possibility that banks and **analysts tend to cover** and (are chosen to) ...... Michaely, Roni and Kent L. Womack, 1999, Conflict of Interest and the **Credibility** of ...
finance.wharton.upenn.edu/~rlwctr/papers/0424.pdf

[PDF] The Rodney L. White Center for **Financial** Research Analyst ...
File Format: PDF/Adobe Acrobat - Quick View
by L Fang - 2005 - Cited by 10 - Related articles
analysts tend to cover firms for which they hold favorable views, ...
finance.wharton.upenn.edu/~rlwctr/papers/0507.pdf

⊞ Show more results from upenn.edu

Shifting fortunes: The political economy of **financial** ...
by L Howard - 1997 - Cited by 36 - Related articles
Badly overextended, significantly **compromised** and eclipsed by presidential ..... A survey by industry **analysts Agusto Co., cover**ing 56 banks, ... Consequently, there is no **reliable** data from which to gauge the shift by firms from ...
linkinghub.elsevier.com/retrieve/pii/S0305750X9600085X - Similar

[PDF] WFC **Financial** Instruments Comment Letter
File Format: PDF/Adobe Acrobat - Quick View
Aug 19, 2010 ... and the professional **analysts who actually cover** the industry, all of whom oppose ... These highly subjective valuations will **compromise** the integrity and ..... Accordingly, it is not possible to obtain **reliable** evidence ...
www.fasb.org/cs/BlobServer?blobcol=urldata&blobtable...id...

Competition and Opportunistic Advice of Financial Analysts: Theory ...
by E Sette - 2007 - Cited by 2 - Related articles
of optimism of affiliated **analysts. When more analysts cover** a stock, ... to misreport information and in equilibrium their **credibility** could be **compromised**. ... When recommendations are **credible**, and only the message of the ...
papers.ssrn.com/sol3/Delivery.../SSRN_ID965861_code451678.pdf?...1

Google output in 2010.

UNIT FOUR: Sense-making Through Information Context | Page 4:29

Google   "(analysts | researchers) * cover" ~credible ~compromise intitle:financial

About 30 results (1.24 seconds)

[PDF] **Growth and Risk in Financial Analysts' Stock ...**
https://pdfs.semanticscholar.org/.../bcfb4f586b9ab3b29a1887375a008213... ▼
compromise between (1) having enough observations to avoid excessive ..... services is not large enough (28 observations) for making reliable .... study are driven by firms with high analyst following or by analysts who cover a particularly.

[PDF] **Financial Fraud and Analyst Reputation - Editorial Express**
https://editorialexpress.com/cgi-bin/conference/download.cgi?... ▼
Jan 31, 2014 - credibility of the analyst's forecasts and consequently rely less on her ... by showing that financial analysts, particularly when they compromise .... Therefore, in our empirical analysis below, we focus on analysts who cover ...

Open PDF in Browser
https://papers.ssrn.com/sol3/.../SSRN_ID2924661_code102678.pdf?...1...
We also provide evidence on several plausible mechanisms through which industry ...... compromise analysts' willingness to be effective monitors if their monitoring may ..... Average number of firms followed by analysts that cover the.

[PDF] **Industry expertise and monitoring effectiveness of financial ...**
www.fmaconferences.org/Orlando/Papers/analystmonitoring.pdf ▼
by D Bradley - 2015 - Cited by 12 - Related articles
relationship could compromise analysts' willingness to be effective monitors if their monitoring may .... "Conflict of interest and the credibility of underwriter analyst ...... Average number of firms followed by analysts that cover the subject firm.

The same query in 2019. Note the diminishing presence of related articles, academic citations, and the disappearance of the cascading "Show more like this or "- Similar" articles from referring links.

Discussion Points

- With the advent of social media, this kind of trend-watching is becoming more widespread and applied to smaller, discrete groups. Rather than income, race, or age, all one needs are the collective histories that enjoin us in our social networks.
- What kind of history? As investigators we should aim our search target sites on the fixations and passions of first parties. Any obsession will do – especially a common interest that clarifies and isolates the priorities of a single issue, shared interest, or common threat.
- How do we leverage third parties as the standard-bearers for credibility? The more active version of third parties involves observers who deliberately keep their professional distance from the first parties they assess. Research organizations, rating agencies, and government oversight functions, for example, are third parties whose influence is determined by how credibly they maintain their independence from the leaders and organizations they evaluate. The moment that distance is impugned by a conflict of interest, they lose their independence as well as their authority.
- Can we as investigators rig the deck? 'Course not. We can no more speak for third parties as we can effectively arbitrate on brokering the best programs, most influential networks, or visionary leaders. What we can do is tap our query formation tools to track the arguments being made and the opinions being swayed. What we can do is measure the messages sent by first parties and those sent by second parties. Want a formula for credibility? It's there in this comparison.

Credibility is about Independence

We often overhear how certain messengers and public figures see their reputations and fortunes rise and fall according to their credibility. In this light, a provider's ability to be taken at their word, in fact taken seriously at all, is based on the highly intuitive choices we make to pay attention to or tune out from what the messenger is providing us.

With so many competing messages and channels for receiving them, credibility is not just a stronger hand for making speeches or taking positions. It is a precious asset that information providers forfeit at their own peril.

Credibility for Message Receivers

Investigators share this critical dependence on the virtue of being credible. To lose credibility is not just to be perceived as less knowledgeable or attention-worthy. It is an indictment on the investigator's judgment – our critical ability to process events and analyze outcomes. Our analysis runs independent of how this impacts the persons and groups standing to gain or lose from the conclusions we reach.

Independence is not only critical to an investigation. It is often the only factor working in favor of the investigator. That's because the players we engage through our web searches and subsequent interviews will regard us as complete strangers – not only to them personally. It's also to the loyalties they may be honoring with their actions.

The most effective way to be less invasive or threatening? Come to the table with an open mind. Easy enough? Not exactly.

Often our background research or cursory understandings lead us to harbor suspicions that preclude alternative explanations or more complete understandings. These instinctual perceptions are a huge threat to our credibility. The last way we want our interviews to go is for the entire discussion to be about what we investigators intend to do with the information we're given. That guarantees two outcomes: (1) inaccurate and/or misleading statements from, (2) folks who have little to say about subjects they know entirely well.

That's why the background work we do prior to direct questioning of a witness, expert, or potential team member is foundational to the success of the investigation. It's not that search engines find us the guilt, innocence, or suitability of the folks we google first before we meet. It's that our web investigation is the strongest case we can make for our own credibility because:

1. An expanded knowledge of our search targets keeps the focus away from ourselves; and
2. Exposure to the differing views within our PCF helps us to keep perspective (and a healthy distance from the issue in question)

The second point is all the more critical when we're called in 'to keep tabs on someone' or inform a decision based on the need for *closer* scrutiny.

- When do thoughts *not* occur to us?
- When do we believe invalidated evidence?

Typically, it's not when we're drawing in that evidence but when we're drawing unsupportable conclusions. We're rushing to judgment when we shouldn't be rushing or judging. The more we identify with a victim or a cause, or a policy position, the more we compromise our effectiveness to lead or manage independent investigations.

There is perhaps a third point for using credibility to keep us researchers honest and on track. And it goes like this: We don't compromise the evidence by oversimplifying issues or fixating on a single person or party.

That's the need to thread together our people and topic searches. Our web investigation should set its sights on search targets that include both people and the ideas that galvanize them. It's rare that we will ever focus exclusively on an individual, or say, a public policy. In fact, often when we hit a failsafe, it's because we've failed to balance the larger social dimension of an elusive person or the personal aspects of a broad policy issue. Both targets support the overall research aim. For example, we witness...

- Irregularities in how an executive handles their company's operations
- How a criminal network perpetrates hoaxes, scams, and frauds on unsuspecting consumers

CREDIBILITY AS SOCIAL DYNAMIC

So what happens when the credibility questions shifts back to the information provider? First of all, researchers are compromised when we're considered actors or participants in the cases we're trying to uncover. Secondly, we want to find search targets that share the same need for perspective that we do. That doesn't mean we both share the same understandings, knowledge, or perspectives. It simply means they can see the people and topics we pursue from both a vested and detached perspective.

Where do we find such people?

Perhaps an ideal blend of direct experience and elevated perspective exists with former employees. Members of an extended social network like LinkedIn may be willing to talk about their past encounters with our search targets. They are speaking from first-hand accounts of the person's job performance, sense of team play, and even their personal quirks and work habits. The level of candor increases in these situations precisely because ex-employees are free from the threat of reprisals or political infighting that results from (1) exposing a colleague, or (2) voicing opinions that would otherwise attract public attention to a private matter.

This kind of impunity can also be found on a group level where organizations are largely self-supporting. Also, its members are brought together through a more sustaining purpose than individual financial gain. A phrase like "one of the most influential organizations you've never heard of" draws a compelling picture of a group whose effectiveness is based on a *mission* or higher calling. Such groups carry more credibility because they are free of the need to keep up a public appearance. Most commercial success is dependent on public recognition. Hence, the need to attract attention through marketing or lobbying efforts.

Grounded (and Unfounded) Suspicions

When do we know credibility is in short supply? When do we need to sprout our antennas to pick up the credibility signals that others miss? That depends in large part on who's doing the talking and who they're communicating to. A dead giveaway that the hounds are on the prowl? When we come across requests for anonymity in the media. This tells us that either the information provider...

- Is talking to imaginary people and making the whole thing up, or themselves, or
- An insider has the need to make a statement they can't bring themselves to stand behind for fear of facing legal retribution or the angry mob with pitchforks assembled outside their corner office

Going on the record could mean our whistleblower is...

- A person of strong character and integrity
- Surrendering names to authorities in the hope of getting leniency in their sentencing
- Disclosing a selective version of past events to distract investigators from other details they wish to remain suppressed
- All of the above

The Candor of Strangers

Our more savvy friends and business contacts know where to find our buttons and how to push them. They know how to curry favor, sing our praises, or even voice their displeasure that grabs our immediate attention. But when perfect strangers exchange their views, their opinions pack an impact that the folks we know really can't match. Ever find yourself talking to a total stranger on an airplane?

Assuming this is a one-time meeting, they have no incentive to tell us anything but the unvarnished truth about how we appear, or what they perceive about us. Impersonal intimacy happens in the virtual world when we inspire total strangers to post responses on our Facebook pages, or engage us on discussion boards. It's not the ulterior motives of those in our networks but the power of an idea that helps us see buttons we are pressing, without even knowing it – and then – boom! Out of nowhere a dialog ensues about how someone else relates to what we're sharing.

The Guise of Celebrities

Unlike that stranger slumped into seat 22C on your last flight, celebrated newsmakers like entertainers and athletes operate within the staged distortions of the public spotlight. Our BS detectors must be calibrated to the amplification of otherwise mundane asides. These trivial personal details become bold social declarations when the media juxtaposes an absent-minded comment with the macro trend it reinforces: Think male politicians referring to the female reporter at the press conference as 'sweetheart.' The upshot? A Knowledge-ABLED investigator cannot take celebrity interviews at face value because of the potentially explosive nature of these off-the-cuff comments.

And it's not just the whiff of scandal that our BS sniffers are sensing in these public displays. The intent to diffuse controversy or disarm a potential adversary is no less a distortion than a less-than-innocent gaffe. Here are some potential signs that an on-the-record exchange reflects the back-channel coaching our celebrated witness received than the actual transcripts we're reviewing:

1. **Intimacy** – The celebrity confides something to this drone reporter he would never spill on the lap of the competing story producer.
2. **Regret** – The big name embraces the faceless reporter as a confidante – not just a mere immortal cigar-puffing hack.
3. **Gratitude** – The star is uncomfortable conferring credit unto himself and directs the reporter to give his teammates equal billing. Deities of choice may rank even higher.
4. **Uncertainty** – Nothing is less natural for a drone reporter than to detect an air of uncertainty. The planting of doubt in all its tortured forms bears the very seeds of authenticity. It's the unresolved aspects of twists and turns that made great narratives in the past and in the foreseeable future.

SOURCING CREDIBLE REFERENCES

Don't go to the source. Go to the recipient. That's the rule for raising the credibility factor in our investigations. What am I getting at here?

Up until now, we've viewed the roles and responsibilities of second parties as reporters or agents for transferring the knowledge and affairs of first parties to third party publics and constituencies. They have another common, well-defined, and sincere role to play as receivers of first party goods and services. Yes, second party buying groups are customers too.

Who has our attention when we research a big ticket item and solicit authority opinions? Is it the supplier of the product? Is it the supplier's rivals or the broader industry they belong in? Vendors and the segments they compete in express views of themselves that are by definition self-serving, at best questionable, and more times than not, self-selecting.

Why is this a more credible position than what reporters provide? Customers are waging actual dollars by staking their fortunes to those of their suppliers. That kind of commitment is certainly more binding than the heresy of a second party reporter, or analyst who might not even use or understand the products they're retained to publicize.

Former U.S. Defense Secretary Robert Gates summed up the same sincerity rationale succinctly in the the aftermath of the WikiLeaks controversy in 2010 when he said:

> "The fact is governments deal with the United States because it's in their interest, not because they like us, not because they trust us, and not because they believe we can keep secrets."
>
> – Farhan (2010)[4]

LATERAL THINKING AS A CREDIBILITY CHECK

Lateral thinking is an approach to problem-solving where an indirect response provides the best answer.[5] Being one step removed from an information source removes the firsthand bias that compromises the perceptions of first persons and parties. We see this in our focus on credibility as the gold standard for assessing the quality of the evidence we're reviewing.

We can apply lateral thinking to our investigations when we do the following:

1. Blend firsthand experience (authenticity) and third-party observation (credibility) by focusing on second persons or second parties with direct (personal) experience of your primary search target.

2. Recognize that those with direct experience look at those individuals (our targets) through the performance of services and actions – not through self-promotion, self-referential words, or purchased endorsements.

UNIT FOUR: Sense-making Through Information Context | Page 4:35

The best way to trust the judgments we hear is to 'walk across the block' or extrapolate who stands to gain/lose from its investment in our search targets.

In that spirit, from a PCF perspective, consider these ground rules:

1. Always start from the premise that there is an interdependent relationship between first and second parties
2. Hear from an industry that enjoys a symbiotic link to the one in question
3. Examples of the most reliable (credible) sources to use when we're assessing an investigation target include these anchoring perspectives: Are they observers, participants and how vested are they in the outcomes of the targets they're tracking?

FIGURE 4.13: Symbiotic Relationships for Sourcing Credibility

Supplier (First Party)	Recipient (Second Party)
1. Public company profiles	Investment securities firms
2. Regulatory battles	Trade associations
3. Household appliances	Electric utilities
4. Retailers	Credit card issuers
5. Media	Advertising agencies / leading advertisers
6. Airlines	Hotels
7. Construction	Real estate
8. Consumer electronics	Batteries
9. Road food / highway construction	Truck drivers

Conjugating the Verbiage

The nine instances shown in Figure 4.13 above reinforce lessons drawn from the following materials:

1. Steps that involve combining search tools and source groupings, introduced in **Units Two** and **Three**
2. Ways to see through the dynamics of the message senders and recipients we've identified through provider conjugation, introduced here in **Unit Four**
3. Expanding our proficiency in interpreting and leveraging information sources according to their credibility and vested interests as information providers

Extrapolation in Action

We all know the cliche about elected leaders speaking their minds in public...

> *Question: What's the first signs that our politicians are not being entirely candid?*
>
> *Answer: When their lips move.*

We all know that banks get robbed because that's where the money is – even by their own bankers. Our powers of BS detection are tested and strengthened each day when elected officials, corporate leaders, and attention-starved celebrities keep two separate ledgers: (1) their words, and (2) deeds.

The paper-based journalism industry may never recover. But exposing hypocrisy is as much a winning business model as a self-protective impulse that keeps our *honest* doubts in line with our *reasonable* expectations.

So how do we keep our BS detectors in working order during our techie research missions? After all, there's so much to sift through that the volume of pros and cons overwhelms those vows we make to stand our middle ground. To see the trade-offs from false choices. To map those choices to our business, our values, our clients. Period.

In the technology business, it helps to lower the degrees of separation from trade show evangelists to the unassuming functional managers. BS levels drop when we're dealing with working stiffs, e.g. middle managers like me. That's because we don't seek the victory of a sales closing. We crave the solace of living within our system choices. That doesn't mean anyone manning the trade show booth has a used car they want to pawn off on those walking the hall.

But it does mean that the folks who earn their keep by holding costs down care more about war stories than case studies. They care about the unexpected experience than the full feature list. They couch those potential conflicts less in terms of how the program works and more in terms of the peers they'll have to work with. They are not looking outside for recognition, but within their organizations for the internal approval needed to pull resources and manage the project.

The Limits of Provider Conjugation

So far we've applied the PCF to each of the roles and situations that impact the sending and receiving of individual and group-based communications. We've reviewed this in terms of typical situations, dynamics and behaviors that occur within first, second, and third person and party contexts.

This model is useful – to a point. As we saw in souring credible references, PCF is key to ascribing motivations to senders and receivers alike. It's an excellent tool for measuring the self-interest of the message sender against the perceptions and sometimes conflicting agendas of those it reaches.

But PCF has the potential to create more confusion than it explains because it is context-dependent. We may be members of a trade association with inside knowledge of how a sister member from a separate industry operates. We might also be an individual consumer who makes purchases independently of whether or not that benefits our employer or the other trade group members. Sounds a bit dense, no?

The problem is that most of us dependent spirits take actions on behalf of ourselves and the groups we represent. Trying to untangle these arrangements would be challenging under the simplest arrangements and the most acute record-keeping. If a message is communicated in public, can we automatically assume it's a façade or intended to mislead a gullible set of recipients? Conversely, can we assume a conflict of interest if we later learn that an internal debate around that communication was hotly contested? No, we cannot put our own fears and suspicions above the body of evidence we're evaluating.

The upshot? Provider Conjugation makes sense to use in fixed, recurring situations where the roles are well-established and the rules of engagement are understood by all participants. For more fluid situations where the characters are harder to cast, the outcomes are more uncertain, and the ambiguities outweigh the absolutes, we apply another contextual tool – the Vectors of Integrity.

Analyzing Context: The Vectors of Integrity

- What is an integrity vector?
- How is this different than provider conjugation?
- Where and when do we apply it to validate the findings in our research?

When we first assessed some common information exchanges in the PCF model, we assigned information attributes to the motivation vectors of those exchanges. We looked at opposing forces that are neither uniformly positive or negative factors. Both feed the context of the evidence communicated in our investigations.

Two seminal and opposable forces we considered were credibility and authenticity. We also contrasted precision and comprehensiveness, loyalty and skepticism, etc. Independently, each factor sounds desirable. Can a researcher be too comprehensive in their research? Can an investigator really have too much credibility in their findings?

Well ... um ... in fact, yes.

It's not exactly that any body of knowledge yields an excessive and unhealthy dose of credibility. It's that the detachment it conveys requires the counterweight of authenticity in order to be both: (1) believed, and (2) acted on. Credibility on its own lacks the realism that can only be captured through a shared and vested interest riding on a tangible and specific outcome. Otherwise, it's too abstract. It's removed from the actual people that an exceedingly credible decision will impact.

That's where integrity strides in to vet the evidence we collect, the arguments that tunnel under our skin, and the doubts we face as second-hand witnesses to the persons, institutions, and records we investigate.

Integrity of Character

Think of a soldier-turned-politician who advocates for peace – someone who's lived firsthand what most of us can only invoke through metaphor and delusion. That's a person of impeccable experience and observation. Unlike the uncomplicated stereotypes we used in the PCF, our statesman example is not mapped to the extreme of either vector but rooted in the center.

He reflects back on his life in the balance when the bullets flew first-hand. But he also knows the need for protocol and temperance. He knows that passion around the negotiating table can be as much a liability to negotiation as going into battle without a weapon.

Now let's revisit some of those plot points we introduced in the earlier vectors. Where or how could integrity be located in the cross-roads of the following continuums? Here are the nine pairings:

FIGURE 4.14: The Vectors of Integrity

1. Authentic ←	→ Credible
2. Experiential ←	→ Observational
3. Loyal ←	→ Skeptical
4. Active ←	→ Deliberative
5. Strategic ←	→ Tactical
6. Structured ←	→ Flexible
7. Original ←	→ Tested
8. Precise ←	→ Comprehensive
9. Expedient ←	→ Exhaustive

The Political Dartboard

Now let's break it down into something real. Since we started out with our war hero statesman, let's stick with the same prism for applying integrity vectors in a sphere of influence even the most apolitical among us have a hard time escaping. The analogy is especially useful in the United States, given the country's two party political system which reduces the complexities of all policy issues to a single binary lens of:

5. Public or private
6. Red state or blue state
7. Caucasion or *of color*
8. For us or against us, etc.

If we look at the creeping influence of cable news channels, we see an accepted and instructive narrative in the undercurrent of nearly every news story. It's home team versus away team. It's Republican against Democrat. It's the right and left punching each other out in sound-bytes and competing narratives. Heroes and scapegoats are assigned credit and blame for the 'sound' policies they craft and promote and the 'failed' policies they trash and try to repeal.

Even political leaders who lack charisma or good debating skills can seize the limelight when the trashing becomes personal. The less principled and consistent the stances taken, the easier it is to cast the petty aspersions than to debate the great issues. But it's simpler to size up the person than to determine the future merits of an abstract policy. And it's certainly easier to spool campaign cash into ads that communicate on those terms. **(Frum, 2012)**[6]

On the political playing field, authenticity stems from absolutism. Staking out an absolute position is the equivalent to an exclusive showing of a house, an official sponsorship of an event, or an original work that can't be duplicated. Absolutism is on display in maniacal quests to be President, i.e. the *severity* of Governor Mitt Romney's conservatism in the 2012 Republican primaries. Positions on issues are rearranged around this priority, pretty much to the exclusion of the others (or that of future primary seasons).

From a policy perspective, that's what's known as a flip-flop. But from a character perspective, that's genuine authenticity. His accusers label him a fake because all his convictions dwell within this single aspiration. He can always rework whatever he rationalizes in public. Are his convictions baseless? Not if his resolute wish to be President forms the basis of his public life. That's fair game for satirists, historians, journalists, and ultimately voters. PCFs won't tip the election or even cast a judgment – other than we need to consider our political candidates as individuals, and as leaders, and decide: Can we live with the contradictions formed by these often diverging identities?

INTEGRITY VECTORS

Now let's apply the generalities of political reporting to each of the vectors. For each diametrical force, we will consider how integrity straddles the center, drawing strength from the extremes but not their excesses.

As we're about to see, each indicator in Figure 4.14 includes a range (continuum) to plot active and passive behaviors (observational and experiential vectors). Each continuum forms the context. What does that context tell us?

1. How integrity embodies the virtues of each opposable force, and
2. How its absence leads to an imbalance, posing a compromising influence of those same forces

Evidence our first indicator: The agenda vector.

VECTOR:	OBSERVATIONAL	EXPERIENTIAL
AGENDA:	Take nothing at face value	Take no prisoners

1) Authentic Versus Credible

Authentic candidates are seen as genuine and emotionally honest (if not steadfast in their beliefs). A candidate lacking authenticity is perceived as artificial, appearing more fickle and sensitive to the political winds than their own convictions and principles. But as we have seen in our PCF travels, pure authenticity can blind messengers who are completely beholden to their own subjective experience. Conversely, a credible messenger is open to a broad range of inputs and opinions. But a well-rounded perspective is an empty one, devoid of direct experience and personal connection.

Vector Positioning: Integrity stakes out the middle of the integrity vector. A person of integrity keeps enough distance from a decision to see the motivations and perspectives of clashing parties. But that distance is not so remote or *safe* that it's based on secondhand or purely observational evidence.

VECTOR:	OBSERVATIONAL	EXPERIENTIAL
Professional Virtue:	Credible	Authentic

2) Experiential Versus Observational

This is the old argument that one story is worth a thousand words – or perhaps a million numbers. For instance, it's easier for people to open their hearts (and wallets) when adversity can be personified through the bloated belly of a famished orphan. That's the subjective experience of suffering. It's raw and emotional, naked, and real. It's a mere drop in the quantifiable bucket of the ravages of poverty. But if our brains are told that five million African children go to bed hungry, guess what? That abstraction doesn't measure up to response drawn from the illustration of the personal – the indelible immediacy of one person's plight. (University of Oregon Study)[7]

At first glance, this makes no sense, says Jonah Lehrer, the author of **How We Decide:**

> "We should give away more money when we are informed about the true scope of the problem, not less. Why do we do this? The depressing statistics leave us cold, even when they are truly terrible."

And yet, concludes Lehrer, the good news is that we're still wired to care about each other:

> "We feel pleasure when someone else feels better."

Vector Positioning: The balancing of experience and observation is very much a balancing act. In his book **Adaptive Leadership**, Ronald Heifetz talks about the two perspectives that uphold our notion of integrity – the need for a simultaneous presence on: (1) the figurative dance floor and, (2) balcony of the public arena:

> "The 'balcony' (looking down on the 'dance') is where you get a larger perspective of what you're facing and how you are doing with your response. From here you do your observing of patterns, reflecting, option thinking, analyzing and monitoring of the change. When you take action and make an intervention, you have stepped onto the 'dance floor' and are participating in the dance. For example, you convene a meeting, announce a strategy, create a task force, restructure, and reassign some staff." **(Heifetz, 2009)**[8]

The point, Heifetz maintains, is that one needs to switch between roles – often with little warning and certainly without the time needed for full deliberation or engagement.

VECTOR:	OBSERVATIONAL	EXPERIENTIAL
Orientation:	Objective	Subjective

3) Loyal Versus Skeptical

Skeptical candidates are analytical creatures. They prioritize consistency of logic and credibility over faith and commitment. Loyalists stick to their hunches, espousing allegiance over skepticism, and action over deliberation. Loyalists are seen as pledged to authenticity virtue – even when the surfacing facts fly against the broader strategy that carries familiar and oft-repeated arguments and rationales.

Vector Positioning: Integrity insists on proof. It doesn't offer unconditional buy-ins for plans or rationales because they sound plausible or curry favor. But once proven, integrity holds to the conviction required to serve higher principles, at the expense of personal gains and self-preservation.

VECTOR:	OBSERVATIONAL	EXPERIENTIAL
Personal Virtue:	Skepticism	Loyalty

4) Active Versus Deliberative

A person of action wants their deeds to speak louder than their oratory or their intellect. Decisive commanders express confidence in their decisions and rarely look back. Action-based leaders favor a one-sided approach: Goal-oriented, sometimes to the exclusion of ambiguous feedback and dissenting views.

Deliberative leaders are more reflective, characterized by a process-oriented approach for reaching consensus, compromise, and resolution. They revisit past decisions and leave prior commitments open to question and revision, accused of indecision or saddled with *paralysis through analysis.* Integrity seeks a balance of planning and execution so that whatever unplanned outcomes result can be addressed – even after the initial plan is carried out.

Vector Positioning: Integrity blends the urgency to move forward with the willingness to take informed risks. Decisions are not impulsive and information-gathering serves a purpose. Collection is not for the sake of collecting. Listening is not to strike a thoughtful pose but to give fullest consideration.

VECTOR:	OBSERVATIONAL	EXPERIENTIAL
Process:	Analysis	Action

5) Strategic Versus Tactical

One common continuum used by students of leadership is the interdependency between the grand designs of strategy and the concrete steps of tactical advancement. In our earlier **Unit One**-based SPM model we see this trade-off in the relationship between purpose (the *why* in search project management) and objectives (the 'where' we're going aspect of SPM).

In politics, the strategist is the statesman – the analytically-inclined visionary who tends to favor strategies based on 'big picture thinking' and their global implications – even to the point of grandiosity. The opposing vector is held by the political operative. Operatives are the infantry. They are the boots on the ground in political turf battles. They focus on clear and present objectives and rarely stray from actions that trigger fixed and measurable returns.

Vector Positioning: Integrity seeks to stretch boundaries without pushing too far too fast. Cutting a deal must be based on: (1) the enlightened self-interest of opposing parties with *skin in the game*, and, (2) enough face-saving to provide political cover for the ground ceded by opposing parties.

VECTOR:	OBSERVATIONAL	EXPERIENTIAL
CONTRACT:	Investments & Partnerships	Pacts & Oaths

6) Structured Versus Flexible

Structured is a looser construct for the more politically-charged *ideological*. It means that candidates see the world through a lens that gives consistency to their decisions. It injects an air of probability to anticipated responses of future events as they unfold. Structured leaders are often commanding in their leadership, especially when that candidate enjoys widely favored position. This position shields him from attack. A more precarious position describes traditionally sensitive *no-win* issues where the candidate is vulnerable for asserting any position.

Flexibility expands the range of options and the uncertainties that come with them. Flexible decision-makers engage in dissonant and complex issues. This pits them in the role of conciliator and broker of clashing parties. Flexible leaders are attentive listeners. However, a full appreciation for the stakes (and potential downsides) faced by competing interests poses additional risks to conciliators. They will be accused of abandoning the people, causes, and reneging on the commitments that first brought them to power.

Vector Positioning: A middle ground between these two extremes would blend the two-way dialog of more flexible thinking with the one-sided determination of the structured approach. The integrity of the two means a process-oriented style for reaching consensus, compromise, and resolution. There is no surrender to one's principles or the deal-breakers deemed to be off the negotiating table.

VECTOR:	OBSERVATIONAL	EXPERIENTIAL
POSTURE:	Impartial	Committed

7) Original Versus Tested

One of the most convincing ways a leader can play both sides of the authentic versus credibility card is to portray the role of the 'original' – someone who can't be held to the traditional rules of political gravity because *the mold was broken when they made [blank]*. That introduces the element of destiny to an otherwise routine checklist of candidate foibles and tendencies.

Originals are also Rorschach Tests – blank canvasses where voters can project their aspirations and desires for a better future. By design, these candidacies are untested. The intrusion of an actual track record steals the romance from incumbent candidates. The devil-you-know counterclaim? At least we know what we're getting.

Vector Positioning: Integrity doesn't dismiss the realities of the recent past nor the possibilities of a foreseeable future. How willing it is to honor the history and uphold the promise depends on how those understandings are reached. In this case, the two opposable forces on the vector are either legalistic and documentable, or more loyalty-based and confidential.

VECTOR:	OBSERVATIONAL	EXPERIENTIAL
WORLDVIEW:	"This is a complicated issue"	"This is a dangerous place"

8) Precise Versus Comprehensive

Precision is not in the engineering world where math calculations are peer reviewed and repeatable to the satisfaction of other practicing experts. In the rhetorical world, precision means striking nerves. Sometimes it's fact-based. But the evidence is highly selective and the delivery is equally important, hinging on the vocal inflection of the speech or sound byte it dwells in.

A comprehensive message is selling its attention to detail and the many ways a series of actions may play out in due course. Often the comprehensive pitch loses the comprehension of its intended audience. The need to *cover all bases* with its attention to process and method often clouds over the clear outcomes a comprehensive approach is intended to deliver.

Vector Positioning: Integrity doesn't over-rely on first impressions, gut instincts, or an inflated sense of its own judgments of character. But it doesn't farm out its bidding and jawboning to surrogates. An agreement without an emotional commitment is a hollow one, and prone to the rewrites of unreliable circumstances.

VECTOR:	OBSERVATIONAL	EXPERIENTIAL
OUTCOME:	Permission	Trust

9) Expedient Versus Exhaustive

There's the side that takes up arms. There's not a moment to waste or a resource to squander. And then there's the side that takes up time, digging in their dragging heels until the clock winds down. There's the force for change and the countervailing force of resistance.

The maniacal focus of journalists to referee these conflicts can compromise their judgment. Linguist Deborah Tannen calls this "a single-minded devotion to balance [that] creates the illusion of equivalence where there is none." **(Tannen study)**[9]

Political campaigns are all about two things. One (money) gets the glory and the other (timing) is scarcely mentioned. But it's through the scheduling that campaigns can revive neglected issues or recast and direct long-simmering resentments in newfound ways. Issue avoidance can lull voters into a false sense of security, just as a jarring recurrence can trigger a reflexive backlash. It is the wild card of unforeseeable events that force the hand of the best-laid campaign plans. It's the severity of external pressures that drive internal adjustments to the timing, emphasis, and pacing of campaign messages.

When to turn up the heat of campaign rhetoric, lower it, or turn it on in the first place? These are questions traditionally addressed in focus groups and phone polling. However, in the social media landscape, these scenarios can be factored into the temperature of hot button issues within any given location and electoral cycle.

A web-based sample of information providers can be used to gauge relationships, character perceptions, and the issues that frame them according to stakeholder perspectives. This wide-ranging group includes civic groups, advocates, enforcement agencies, commentators, media outlets, ad placements, and campaign forums. Regardless of the political turf or the interest of each player, there is a conjugal exchange to be mapped, and ultimately measured through our **Unit Four** modeling techniques.

Vector Positioning: When does Integrity cross over from the fact-finding and dot-connecting to close ranks behind a course of action? Typically that precipice is reached when our investment outweighs any second-guessing or foreseen doubts that would cause us to turn back or disown our own conclusions or decision-making.

VECTOR:	OBSERVATIONAL	EXPERIENTIAL
FINAL STATEMENT:	Draws conclusions	Makes decisions

The Verdict on Vectors

The occupation with politics and heads of state are not meant to limit all illustrations to its hyper-conflicted portrayal on cable news and Twitter. Politicians are but one form of celebrity that invites endless speculations between (1) what public figures say in prepared statements, and (2) how those posturings square with the unscripted, authentic selves that can only exist off-camera.

Relationship vectors are not some truth serum that uncovers falsehoods and seeds of corruption. They're a diagnostic tool that helps us to weigh the objective and subjective-based experience of our search targets, even how we're perceived by others in that pursuit.

Vector Positioning: Integrity is the first player to toss their hat in the ring and last player in the room to pick sides. As we saw in the active-deliberative vector, integrity means active listening without being drawn into factional disputes. Observer or participant — which direction do you naturally lean? I bet the answers are as subjective as the circumstances are unique!

VECTOR:	OBSERVATIONAL	EXPERIENTIAL
MEMBERSHIP:	"With us AND against us"	"With us OR against us"

FIGURE 4.15: Summary of Integrity Vectors

MODEL	OBSERVATION	EXPERIENCE
AGENDA:	Take nothing at face value	Take no prisoners
PROFESSIONAL VIRTUE:	Credibility	Authenticity
ORIENTATION:	Objective	Subjective
EXPECTATION:	Skepticism	Conviction
PERSONAL VIRTUE:	Skepticism	Loyalty
PROCESS:	Analysis	Action
CONTRACT:	Investments & Partnerships	Pacts & Oaths
POSTURE:	Impartial	Committed
WORLDVIEW:	"This is a complicated issue"	"This is a dangerous place"
OUTCOME:	Trust	Permission
FINAL STATEMENT:	Draws conclusions	Makes decisions
MEMBERSHIP:	"With us AND against us"	"With us OR against us"

SECTION 4:2 | The Value of Social Information

As we saw in **Unit Three**, the web as an information ocean has a simple ocean surface. It's called Google, or more precisely what is visible (indexed by search engines) or invisible (the **Deep Web**). That surface is what we referred to as the Internet Radar.

Now that we've introduced several analytical tools for evaluating our search results, we will revisit our radars and calibrate them to the settings of the PCF ("Provider Conjugation Framework"). That way we know what we can reasonably expect in managing the Resource-based **Information Types**, first introduced in **Unit Three**'s Project Resources section. Our new PCF tool reveals how far removed our search targets are from the actions under investigation. Moreover, we can apply this not just to targets, but also the actions and outcomes associated with them.

As we saw at the beginning of **Unit Four**, information exchanges are essential to understanding the comfort zones between information sources and recipients. The jarring reality of our radar screens is that many of our most intimate transactions are not only visible to others, but sequestered from us. This partition between what institutions know about us and what we know of ourselves is particularly insidious. It's not in the interest of those institutions to make these details available to us. How does that play out in our contextual frameworks? Actually, the less guarded we are about our personal identities, the more plentiful – and authentic – the information that can be collected for (and against) us.

Earlier in this unit, we looked at information exchange and how this impacts communications between individuals and other individuals, small and larger groups. What we didn't examine was the more daunting exchange between larger groups in communications about individuals. To harken back to our original insights in **Unit One** on blindspots, these communications about us are likely to exclude us. At least without the aid of a highly-skilled forensics expert or First Amendment attorney.

This is not the kind of a blindspot where our dentist tells us to wear out night guards, lest we grind our molars into nubs of their former selves. This is the kind of blindspot where nondisclosure of larger institutions is key to such evidence-gathering. In the case of private industry, that reason is to sell us more of what we want. In the case of governments, it's to protect us from potential enemies of the state. In either case, electronic eavesdropping is as much a given part of digital connectivity as our estrangement from the larger society when we go offline.

This book does not address the risk of our civil liberties or the need for their protection per se. There is nothing in these pages that shows how to hack into a resource, issue a DNS ("Denial of Service") order against blasphemous websites. We don't address staunching the flow of information that spreads far and wide to third parties we cannot verify, trust, or knowingly support. That is a decidedly off-radar form of information usefulness both in terms of its availability, application, and quite frankly, the extent of my expertise.

UNIT FOUR: Sense-making Through Information Context | Page 4:47

USING PCF TO RENDER RADAR SCREENS

In **Unit Three,** we caught a glimpse in Figure 3.36 of the great and sometimes blurry divide between above and below radar of project sources. We saw how genealogical milestones like births and marriages coincided with business and legal transactions like licensing, employment histories, and personal financial assets.

How hard it is to obtain these records is not a matter of subjective experience. It's evolving policies and technologies that cause the continual shifting of boundaries between what lies above and below radar. The lines drawn between personal and private are in constant flux. They depend on state regulations, court rulings, and the ability of marketers to mine the usage patterns and data trails of web consumers.

We can use PCF to model the inferential line that exists between public and private communications. As the mapping below indicates, that shifting radar floats on the backs of second persons and parties. Quite simply, it all boils down to this: Now that I know, am I a reservoir or a vessel — a container or a conduit? Do I sit on this information or pass it on?

FIGURE 4.16: Mapping Provider Conjugation to What's on or off the Radar

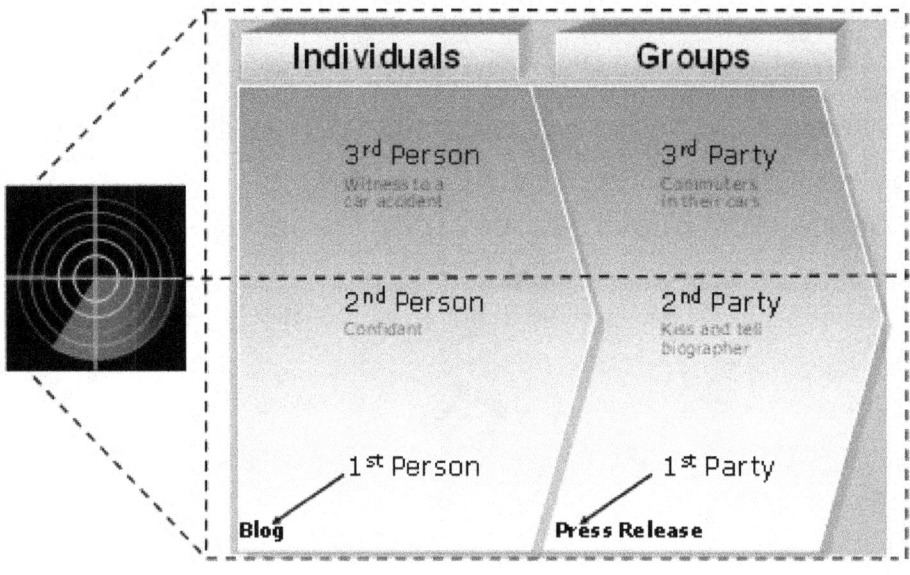

On/off radar is a simple distinction between what is documented and what happens beyond recall. Neither of these groupings is static although the more communications that are conducted electronically the likelier they move from the undocumented to documented column.

What does this mean for us as communicators and the extent of our participation? How does this influence our choice of communication for...

- Introducing ourselves to friends of friends?
- Delivering bad news to family members?
- Sending out invites to people who may not remember us?
- Giving a status on a project to a boss several time zones away?

Conversely, how does this change our approach as observers of our search targets? How does the mapping influence our choice of information providers? What are our stakeout positions for anticipating actions, interpreting outcomes, and even comparing notes with other members of our team?

AUTHENTICITY, CREDIBILITY, CONFLICTS OF INTEREST

As we've established in the trade-offs between subjective and objective biases, we can move forward with our PCF mapping. That means placing more confidence that the information we receive is authentic when the source has...

- Firsthand knowledge,
- Personal involvement (first person/party), and
- Direct knowledge of the actions of others.

Likewise, we can be more certain that our evidence is credible when the source has not been personally involved, but has been an outside observer (third person/party).

Conflicts of interest exist when deals are made *under the table*, or when a person or institution tries to buy their way into credibility. It could mean sponsoring the work of third party research firms, laboratories, and other domain experts inclined to produce opinions and reports in their favor.

PCF reveals some common activities relevant to the vetting such conflicts, specifically in legal cases, and generally in most institutionally-sanctioned discovery pursuits.

Watchdogs and Regulators

The formal or institutional way that conflict-of-interest is exposed is through the government intervention and enforcement of public law. However, the powers of regulators are often compromised when they flirt with dramatically higher pay from the firms they're regulating. Rather than expose risks, they disguise them in legalese or bury them under the weight of vague claims or irrelevant details.

The discrepancy here is in stark display on our search logs. The stated objective would be to preserve the public interest so that investors are protected from the short-term gains of a select few. The clashing and unstated purpose would be for regulators to reap financial rewards far greater they could earn on the public payroll. The expectation we would gain as investigators is that the regulator protects those with political clout. Not the interests of the wider, less organized groups their agency is charged to protect.

The notion of checks and balances is the guiding principle for directing the legal authority of regulatory agencies and the public officials who lead them. The hypocrisy created by the need to protect the few at the expense of the many is as likely to be...

- Revealed in empty, oft-repeated statements, as it is to be...
- Discovered by stealth efforts to obscure, hide, or selectively enforce laws on the books.

For example, in late 2007 high ranking public officials would project the belief that the fundamentals of the economy were basically sound. This pretense services the notion that elected leaders answer to expectations in order to preserve order. Preserving confidence, even when that confidence is false is the appeal of the status quo. This appeal often overpowers all attempts to investigate, reveal, and fix the systemic breakdowns that helped foster the meltdown and the full-blown financial crisis that ensued.

We first considered this in **Unit One** *when we looked at the kinds of blindspots we might expect to encounter in our radar detection efforts when investigating institutional or group behavior.*

Smoking Guns and the Whiff of Hypocrisy

We all know when something doesn't smell right. This is when the righteous words don't support the wrongful deed. We tally the unfortunate outcomes against the isolated actions that led us there. And they don't add up. Our sniffers have led us to the doorsteps of hypocrisy. That might sound esoteric like a Greek tragedy. It's a paper we once turned in about a whistleblower who sounded off against a code of silence. In fact, it's one of the most popular and consistent narratives used by the media. It's a well-established journalistic practice to expose corruption by reporting doubts raised from the conflicting evidence between a person's individual deeds and their public statements – typically as a first party leader or group representative.

Everyone has their own reconstruction of events. Everyone has a selective version of what went down. Everyone has their own sniff test for what *doesn't quite smell right*. However, our own testing merits require us to introduce standards that are widely understood and evenly applied. We need to anticipate public, legal, and stakeholder scrutiny. Our protective instincts may suspect underhanded motives. But our better instincts acknowledge the role of our skeptics to responsibly question our conclusions and quite possibly the methods for our investigation. **(Lewis, Einhorn, 2009[10])**

One of the overlooked benefits of web investigations is this. Because they exist in the public domain, our strongest doubters and most skeptical adversaries can literally conduct the same tests and probes that we conduct – and achieve the same results. Arriving at the same conclusions is a completely different matter!

Figure 4.17 models some of the damning circumstances that we can use to test our hunches. Then we can either strengthen or toss out initial impressions of the people and groups we investigate.

Subjective Experience: The Changing Roles of Information Providers

The distinctions between self and group identification is based on some common roles that we all share as senders and receivers. In Figures 4.17 through 4.19, who is cast on which end of the exchange is highly contextual. Below, we see how those perspectives will shift based on who initiates each communication and the chain of reactions it inspires. The most important pattern? Whether those messages are communicated informally from person to person, or officially through group-based or more traditional media channels.

FIGURE 4.17: Mapping PCFs to Individual and Group-based Information Providers

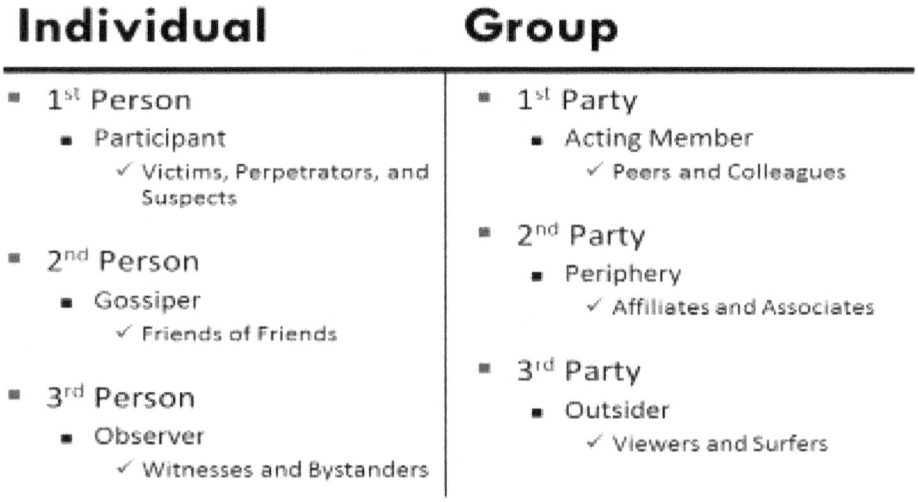

Individual
- 1st Person
  - Participant
    - ✓ Victims, Perpetrators, and Suspects
- 2nd Person
  - Gossiper
    - ✓ Friends of Friends
- 3rd Person
  - Observer
    - ✓ Witnesses and Bystanders

Group
- 1st Party
  - Acting Member
    - ✓ Peers and Colleagues
- 2nd Party
  - Periphery
    - ✓ Affiliates and Associates
- 3rd Party
  - Outsider
    - ✓ Viewers and Surfers

This diagram divides individual and group information exchanges according to the role of the information giver.

Subjective Experience: Information Types and Purposes

In addition to roles and responsibilities, we need to consider the types of information that are exchanged across the PCF playing field. We first addressed this earlier in **Unit Four** when we explored the forms and vestiges of informational artifacts – the physical or electronic containers that store the communication. We expanded the range to include overall purpose for providing information in the absence of a tangible container. Here is a PCF mapping:

FIGURE 4.18: Mapping PCFs to Information Types and Purposes

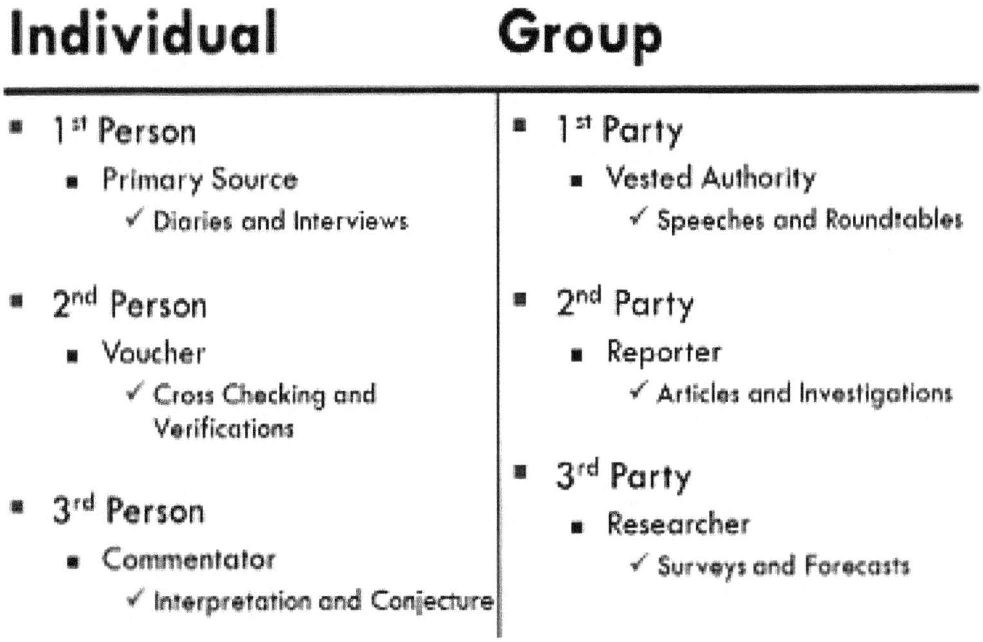

Individual
- 1st Person
  - Primary Source
    - ✓ Diaries and Interviews
- 2nd Person
  - Voucher
    - ✓ Cross Checking and Verifications
- 3rd Person
  - Commentator
    - ✓ Interpretation and Conjecture

Group
- 1st Party
  - Vested Authority
    - ✓ Speeches and Roundtables
- 2nd Party
  - Reporter
    - ✓ Articles and Investigations
- 3rd Party
  - Researcher
    - ✓ Surveys and Forecasts

This diagram divides individual and group information exchanges according to the form and purpose that the information provides us.

UNIT FOUR: Sense-making Through Information Context | Page 4:51

Subjective Experience: On/Off Radar

Consider the flip-side of provider conjugation – it's in the ear of the receiver. The switch happens when we revisit the framework from the perspective of the recipient. The official end of the spectrum floats to the top of the radar. The information or more private side lays low – below the radar. The zig-zag is not an exact calculation so much as a symbol for the slippery task of deciding what information is as likely to float above the surface or remain below.

FIGURE 4.19: Mapping PCFs to their Visibility Across the Internet Radar

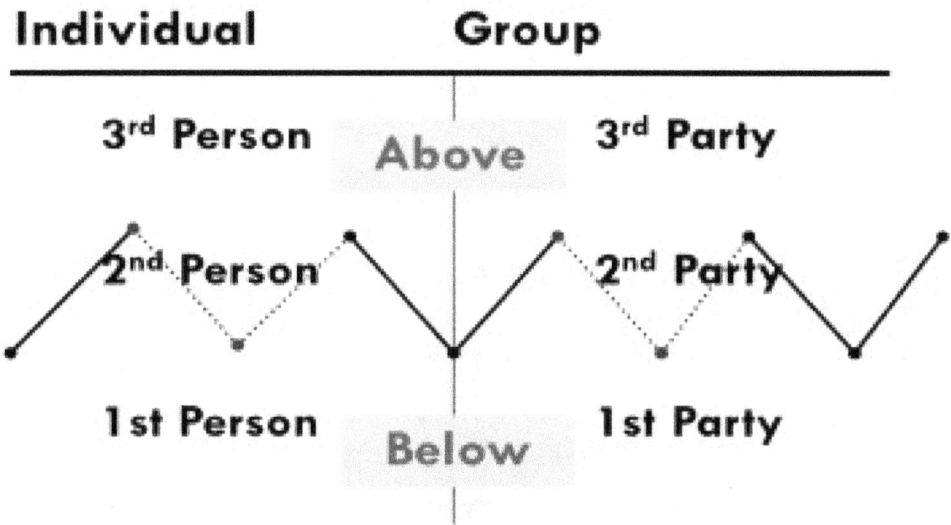

This diagram details the types of information we're exposed to as receivers of information exchanges. It shows the inferential line that exists between public and private communications typified by second person/party information exchanges.

WORKING UNDER THE RADAR

We now have a way of understanding what we reasonably expect to find on screens. We have a new mental model for tracking how information flows and how the direction of that flow will influence the interpretations, perceptions, and potential actions taken by its recipients. We can now see how this contextualization tool is situation-specific. It applies to us and our changing roles as providers or recipients. It also matters whether that communication is compelling us to act alone, or on behalf of a group.

We've also evidenced the limited explanatory powers of PCF in developing tools for analyzing context. That means addressing the numerous and sometimes conflicting forces we all need to reconcile as both providers and recipients. Hence, we've introduced the additional framework of Integrity Vectors to assess these complexities and the range of outcomes our search targets consider as they mull their options and followup actions.

What we haven't done is apply this mental mapping to real life scenarios. We haven't yet considered how to attack the kinds of questions that arise when dissecting a sequence of events, or understanding the underlying motives behind questionable activities. With that in mind, let's put what we've learned to work in the following web investigation:

Working Model: Search Target under Investigation

FIGURE 4.20: Search Target Suspect Profile

Suspect: Profile	Integrity Vectors	PCF Probes
Soloist or orchestrator	Tendency to act alone or in tandem	*Get a handle on socializing patterns through preferred hangouts, elixirs, and emotional range to detect any dramatic behavioral changes*
Exposure settings	Attention-grabbing or quiet (behind-the-scenes player)	*What does an individual or group do to call attention to themselves? When do they shed the limelight? Are they intent on demonstrating their grievances?*
Inspirations	Role models and scapegoats	*Who do they follow on social media settings? What are familiar targets for venting anger or praising – what are those beefs and virtues?*
Motivations	Competitive versus passive nature	*What is target's tendency to initiate communications? How much of their activity streams echo the posts and behaviors of their favored information providers? Are they more passive and likelier to play a supporting role?*
Transparency	Open and available versus secretive and remote	*How elusive or approachable is the target in their social media profiles? Do they attract virtual friends outside their immediate social circles?*

FIGURE 4.21: Search Target Suspect Eccentricities

Suspect: Eccentricities	Integrity Vectors	PCF Probes
Soloist or orchestrator	Temptations and vices	*Factor in past resentments for being passed over nd how those humiliations tempt a mastermind to proclaim their brilliance (and tip their own cover)*
Exposure settings	Perceived slights and vindications	*Consider the scores that were settled in pursuit of false accusations, petty jealousies, and otherwise avoidable past mistakes*
Inspirations	Rituals and habits	*Are there compromising or addictive behaviors that can be traced to social circles or through social media discourse?*
Motivations	Obsessive behaviors, (i.e. history of stalking)	*Does the target obsess on other individuals or groups? Where does the fluid distraction pass into static fixation? If a restraining order were issued, where would the target have crossed the line?*
Transparency	Impersonations, mimicry	*What are the behaviors of the target's heroes and praiseworthy members of the inner circle? When do those praises turn to taunts and ridicule?*

FIGURE 4.22: Search Target Suspect Resources

Suspect: Resources	Integrity Vectors	PCF Probes
Soloist or orchestrator	Expertise to carry out actions	*Take an inventory of financial assets, medical records, membership histories, academic and licensing credentials, and unique talents*
Exposure settings	Assets to finance operation	*Assets to consider from two countervailing angles: (1) What is the risk/benefit calculation for a target determining whether to engage in criminal activities; and (2) What assets need to be protected from potentially hostile actions of perceived adversaries?*
Inspirations	Long-term versus short-term associations	*Does the target share their goal orientation in the conduct of their social media profile? Are their communications more practical and immediate or focused on loftier goals?*
Motivations	Family history of bodily/mental illness	*What are the less-than-natural causes present in the demise of diseased or infirmed family members?*
Transparency	Family ties	*Does the target profile more as family or individually-focused? How much of that decision is based on the real need to break free from the circumstance of their upbringings?*

FIGURE 4.23: Search Target Suspect Network

Suspect: Network	Integrity Vectors	PCF Probes
Soloist or orchestrator	Unhappy investors	*What assets are held (1) within the family, (2) on the periphery by extended members, or (3) intimate confidants outside that circle?*
Exposure settings	Disgruntled employees	*Focus on the enablers — who are the accomplices and go-betweens that function as conduits between the target and actions under investigation?*
Inspirations	Marginalized family members	*What are the weakest links in the family chain? Is the target the n'er-do-well asking for hand-outs? Are they the well-heeled benefactor leaned on for providing bridge loans? Do monetary disputes boil over in estate settlements?*
Motivations	Online forums, discussions	*How does the target perceive themselves Do they command the kind of respect from others that they confer onto themselves? What are they likely to repeat about how they define themselves? Are there any curious disclaimers that connect otherwise unrelated events and outcomes?*
Transparency	Exposure to potential adversaries	*How public is our target about expressing their displeasure and airing their grievances? Are they expressed at specific individuals or do these misgivings take on a more cultural or tribal tone?*

FIGURE 4.24: Search Target Suspect Events

Suspect: Events	Integrity Vectors	PCF Probes
Soloist or orchestrator	Bargaining power	*What's the gap between personal wealth and what's projected in appearances? Where does target show painstaking control and what are they likelier to leave to chance?*
Exposure settings	Upsides and downsides	*Who might gain in prestige and reward from theft, rescue, sale, settlement, etc. Where are the potential blockers to cooperation such as indictment of family member of close friend?*
Inspirations	Expectations range	*What are the target's formative expectations, i.e. groomed as heir apparent? When do they expect to win outside approval or wield some new authority? Are these stepping stones based on privilege, popular will, individual merit, or outright coercion?*
Motivations	Work schedule and personal transactions	*Spot check for calendar events and changes like uptick in work hours. How do scheduling changes impact data trail: Purchase records, cell phone usage, security cameras, browser histories, etc.*
Transparency	Quid pro quos	*Are there back-scratchings, kickbacks, or pre-arrived reciprocal agreements? Is information suppressed to avoid media coverage and public scrutiny?*

SECTION 4:3 | Search to Converse —
How to Socialize What We Learn Through Networking

The social media section of **Unit Four** has two principle thrusts:

1. **Observation** – Approaching social networks as a researcher
2. **Participation** – Engaging them as a member, including how to screen, join, attract, and communicate through virtual communities

The slippery distinction between observer and participant is especially sensitive as we shift from the *searching* to *conversing* phase of our research projects. This section focuses on ways to trail and gather background details on search targets that generate digital identities through their social media profiles, networks, and posts.

The model we use for reading networks and acting on them is called the **Provider Conjugation Framework** or PCF. Like verb conjugation, this tool helps to establish the flow and context of how information travels and the perceptions it carries with it. We also apply it to ourselves as information providers in determining the perceptions we want to form about us. This includes the types of contacts we want to attract and build into our own networks – especially in reaching out to search targets that prove to be social media party animals, digital hermits, or somewhere in-between.

Social networks are important for tracing personal connections such as Facebook friends or LinkedIn connections but impersonal ones too. One's electronic network traces a person's media universe. Those horizons span well beyond access to cable or audio streaming to the experiential realm: Exposure to ideas and cultures that will present choices, and even shape behaviors.

The connection between impersonal information sources and personal decisions and priorities is not a subtle one. What we see, hear and read can influence what we say, think, and act upon. Understanding the electronic environment that surrounds an individual can be just as revealing as their DNA, school grades, and home address. Those influences are felt whether they're delivered through advertising, speechmaking, role models, or fashion statements,

The other direct connection here is that electronic media is our modern equivalent to presenting how society organizes itself into orders, groups, teams, and affiliations. Which of these groups count us as members is often similar to our personal networks. For instance, the sources we subscribe to may be indecipherable from the professional contacts in our smart phones. The causes and crusades that enlist our volunteerism and charity may well represent cures or advocacy for friends and family for which we pledge our unwavering support.

SOCIAL NETS: From Soul Searching to Virtual Searching

Nobody knows...

- The troubles you've seen?
- The trials you've faced?
- The journeys you've tread?
- The secrets you've held?

Certainly search engines are no exception. There is probably no day of reckoning in our lifetimes where search engines will replace confessionals or give psychotherapists cause to switch careers. Disintermediation means cutting out the *middle man* so that buyers and sellers can engage directly. In that context, the web has made mayhem of the career tracks of most travel agents, copy editors, and advertising directors from TV commercials to newspaper classifieds and those yellowing Yellow Pages.

But search engines can inform the question of how we appear as we're stepping and stressing through this world – from everyone else's perspective along the PCF spectrum. And while search won't put the kibosh on people who listen to our problems for a living, it unleashes two opposing forces: (1) It expands our appetite for connections, while (2) constraining pastimes formerly designed for *mixing things up*. It has made lasting changes to how career counselors, headhunters, matchmakers, and event planners design meetings and arrange situations between people and groups. Web-based research is a tool for building bridges and for the cementing of connections made within (1) these meetings, (2) panels they would host, (3) topics they anticipate, and (4) even interviews they might arrange through media covering the event.

Cutting Out the Second Party

Speaking of media, they are on the ultimate endangered list of communicators displaced by web technology, or to be more specific – the emergence of social media on the web. We all know that the infrastructure of our own virtual neighborhoods live on Instagram and Facebook – not in the pages of our local paper. From a PCF perspective, this means the elimination of second parties. Why go through a reporter or a news outlet when political leaders can reach voters directly on Twitter? Why sign with a record label when an established performer can distribute their songs directly to their fans?

We have scarcely begun to understand all the implications stemming from the displacement of second parties. Much has been made about the demise of traditional media and journalistic integrity. Little has been articulated about the opportunity this presents to Knowledge-ABLED investigators to provide the kind of vetting, fact-checking, and quality control services formerly the domain of news reporters. Even less has been written about the role of the Knowledge-ABLED as aggregators to (1) broker contextual meanings, (2) provider credibility, and (3) ultimately the integrity of the search targets and larger social forces they underpin.

But before we consider these downsides and opportunities, we need to focus first on social information: The fundamental (and overlooked) building block of all non-business model social media interaction. Without understanding social information, social media lacks context for us as researchers as well as group members of social networks.

The Role of Social Information

Think about primary intelligence-gathering. A seasoned investigator interviews a key witness. The examiner pays as much attention to the way the answers are delivered as to the answers themselves. Part of this evaluation is based on the source's social network. What are their family roots? Where do they go for a sense of community? Which of their own primary news sources will shape their sense of personal conduct from duty and obligation to individual liberty and social justice?

These are personal values that are woven into that external identity we share as citizens, fans, churchgoers, parents or any group affiliation that tells us the concerns, expectations, and commitments of its members. More than purchase histories and hobbies, the binding nature of personal networks leads the researcher to an unwritten code of priorities and value judgments we refer to as *the social contract*.

Now consider the witness's group affiliations and social circles. What are the key relationships that reinforce, contradict, or raise new questions about what our source decides to share in the interview? Is their version of events compromised by fears of retribution? Is bribery or some other form of coercion requiring them to ignore or downplay the guilt or responsibility of other suspects?

There is but one certainty when it comes to reading through the files of the evidence gathered by an experienced investigator: The relationships conjured up by their interviews weighs as critically as any quote that can be pulled from their interview, debriefing, or legal deposition.

Put another way, whoever we email and cc: on our correspondence, is often as important as the text contained in the body of that message. Who's aware of the issue under discussion is sometimes more critical than the topic itself.

So what exactly is social information? How is that different from social media or social networking? Social information is the context in which information is processed – not created, not delivered – but interpreted. The social value of information stands apart from its objective value as facts, opinions, and details. Social information addresses the subjective judgments and actions formed by the perceptions and values of information recipients.

How does this definition play out in the public spectrum? We'll use traditional media for context.

Traditional Media Bias

When the media is accused of bias, we can guarantee (1) a spirited debate, and (2) the opposite bias harbored in the information provider making the accusation. Left to its own devices, traditional media goes about each story it finds worth covering with the same foregone conclusions:

1. They've done their job correctly if we're still tuned in when the story's over.

2. How they keep our attention is not the lead story when it comes to media bias.

Here are some safe assumptions when learning about the same investigation in the papers, radio or traditional TV news: We're receiving a selective version of events chosen for us by familiar public figures who we have never met before. Their ultimate responsibility is nothing as lofty as an ultimate truth but to capture our attention long enough to sustain their popularity as news providers. Also referred to as secondary sources, we as passive news watchers are privy only to what the show's producer considers broadcast-worthy.

But we are not told how they landed those quotes, who tipped them off, and all those unnamed sources who don't wish to be held accountable for their all-knowing insights. So basically, much of the context or social value derived from the investigation is lost to the news consumer. From a social justice angle, this is a troubling part of news mechanics because a news organization can be subjected to the same coercions as our compromised witness. Only in the case of the news outlet, they are even more vulnerable to outside pressures. They have the added role of deciding not only the public's right to know but, what it, the media, considers worth knowing.

<u>Anti-social Information</u>

Newspapers, magazines, and TV news programs tend to squelch the social dimension of the news they report, on both legal and proprietary grounds. But all the personal networks, group affiliations, and bargaining that goes into deciding what and how to report news is now finding its way into the back corridors of sourcing a hungry investigation. From bloggers to grassroots sites and personal pages, much of the firsthand immediacy and even authenticity is generated by the postings of people with direct ties to investigations, sometimes with case-breaking specifics that would evade traditional news consumers.

Where does this leave us as intrepid Internet researchers? On a personal level, if we've read the blog, what's to stop us from emailing the blogger? What if we are an authoritative source ourselves? What if we've seen the news report? What will the traditional media producer say if we offer a competing version – say to a competing program? Now that the lines between news producers and consumers are blurred, traditional media outlets can ill-afford to pose as the final, definitive arbiters of the news that's fit to print, or the story that's worth watching.

In a broader context, the assessment tools we address in **Unit Four** will bring quantifiable proof to the way search targets and social topics are understood, perceived, and potentially acted on by a full range of information recipients. Increasingly, the web also feeds us full data sets of evidence that are both unfiltered by the providers, and the commentaries of mainstream news organizations. **(Arthur, 2010)**[11]

THE CONCEPT OF SOCIAL CIRCLES

The best way to understand the social dimension of information is through a variation on PCF called **Social Circles**. We can group social circles to map how information travels and what form its documentation takes (indicated by the right-pointing arrows in Figure 4.25). This is the experiential element of information – how it travels and where it lands.

UNIT FOUR: Sense-making Through Information Context | Page 4:61

The distinctions between senders and receivers include the following:

1. An individual or informal social circle represents communication attributed to a specific person.
2. Generally, the smaller the circle, the more sincere and authentic the communication as an extension of a person's individual will, personal preferences, and even *true intentions.*
3. A group-sponsored social circle refers to information provided by organizations, institutions or formally-delivered communications.

Because of their intimacy, core circles are useful for anticipating the upshot or aftermath of a compromising situation or awkward information exchange.

Social circles are also instructive for plotting that most vulnerable posture of all compromised communications – being blindsided. It is a universal reflex and personal affront to loathe learning through the widest of circles what we thought we should be told from a close friend or confidant.

Let's say we want to honor the request of not being blindsided by a boss or authority figure. Now let's assume that this person is busy, overbooked, and easily distracted. Is it better to send them emails directly (e.g., TO: boss) or indirectly (e.g., cc: boss)?

As we see below, social circles are concentrated and intimate at their core and diffuse and impersonal at the periphery. An inner circle is made up of long-time friends, esteemed peers, and contacts we are likelier to lower our guards in exchanging (and safekeeping) personal, off-radar information. We are connected to extended networks for their utility, i.e. suppliers, brokers, partners and other lateral relations share an indirect affiliation. The larger cultural dimensions on the outer layer are abstractions to us. There are no confidences, only perceptions shaped by information providers and forums in the larger social context.

FIGURE 4.25: Subjective Experience in the Form of Social Circles

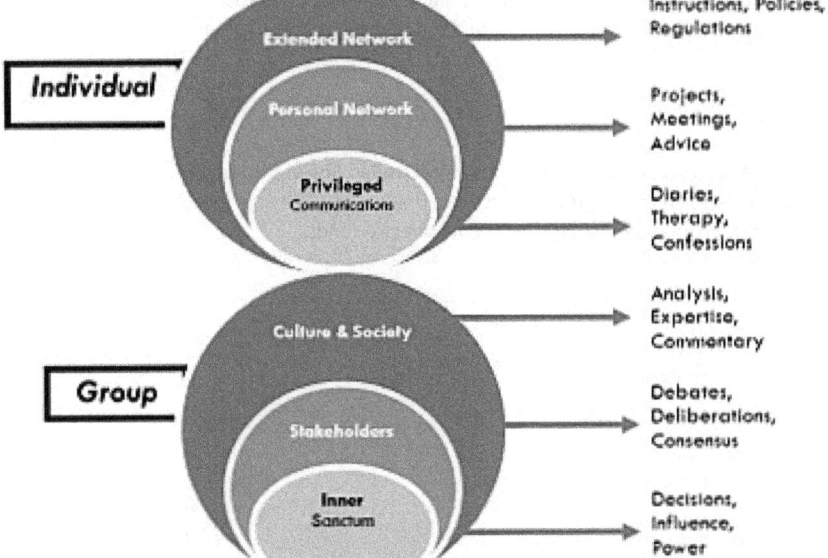

This schematic groups the typical outcomes or by-products of common information exchanges. An individual or informal social circle is attributed to a specific person. A group-sponsored social circle refers to information provided by organizations, institutions or formally-delivered communications.[12]

SOCIAL NETS: From Searching to Conversing

The best virtual display of social circles is through Internet-based social networks. The pre-eminent social network is Facebook and its success at commandeering the attention of its members. This is a bias shared by many of its members who rarely wander off the Facebook ranch – a landlord "which chops infinity into an endless series of cul-de-sacs." **(Tyrangiel, 2010)**[13]

The second kind of social nets are the largely resume-based profiles submitted by professionals looking for new opportunities or looking to reconnect with former colleagues. Professional networking sites get you from the background research of your expeditions to the foreground engagement. This means approaching a key contact with a mutual aim:

1. Our research can help them, and

2. They can move us along in our careers and/or project work.

Professional Networks: LinkedIn

The dominant network for working professionals is currently LinkedIn.com. Unlike Instagram, Facebook, and sites that hold more media clips than career details, LinkedIn is a structured database of interconnected professionals complete with their key credentials, contact details, resumes, and endorsements.

The LinkedIn database is powerful. Remember each detail that it asks of you becomes a searchable field in your quest to find experts, hiring managers, and trade contacts. There is no expectation that we would use the vendor's process for approaching contacts that are more than one degree of separation from us.

Along with the structure, another big selling point is that members invest in their memberships. They spend more time and care in keeping their profiles current than what we might expect to see maintained by a corporate HR department. Endorsements are also welcome and there are built-in safeguards to validate the process. For instance, one can't endorse their own work although we can certainly trade on a quid pro quo with one of our network references. Sound like the laws of credibility calling?

Show You Mine, I'll Show You Yours

So LinkedIn is a massive database of self-administered professional life narratives. Access is determined by a network of click-happy connections: Show you mine if you show me yours (both the resumes *and* the contacts).

The database gets regular feedings and weedings because – hey – those are my bowling trophies and and inflationary job titles and biopic documentaries I put on my reality series reward card program. Psst... got any seed money?

What we're unpacking here through unlicensed metaphor is a database of resumes. The splendor of the architecture is that the profile templates are self-organizing. There are no semantic web quibbles over taxonomies versus folksonomies, what vocabulary is worth controlling, and which tag clouds deserve to float above the fog. In doing so, LinkedIn has achieved organic adherence to the age-old riddle:

> *How do I describe my uniqueness in the least invasive and most universal way possible?*

That vessel is the cross-fertilization of the knowledge garden we researchers, sales animals, and job-seekers can all cultivate, horse-trade, or hunt down. Whatever our motivates, we're sourcing the sprinkler system known as the LinkedIn advanced search feature.

FIGURE 4.26: LinkedIn's Advanced Search Features

One of my favorite applications of PCFs in social networks is the ability to search only former employees of a particular organization. This ensures that the person had firsthand knowledge of what was happening at their former employer.[14]

UNIT FOUR: Sense-making Through Information Context | Page 4:65

The Social Network Mating Dance

Perhaps we don't need to track down ex-employees when investigating the questionable practices of their former firm. Maybe we're looking up people we've lost touch with and want to reconnect? What a concept!

Recently I got pinged on LinkedIn by a former college cohort with a 1.5 separation degree of overlapping concentric social circles circa 1980-84. Who better than a fellow Hampshire College alumn and current job-seeker to put that ivory-coated knowledge harvest to the test?

My former college mate "Jon" writes:

> *So, anyway, I want to harvest some of these connections. At first I thought I'd contact the person I knew, tell them who I was looking for and ask them to search the name and find the second degree connection. A little awkward and time consuming (for the person I'm asking the favor). Yeah, so then I see the "Get Introduced Through A Connection" link. I choose my connection, then I get this form:*

FIGURE 4.27: LinkedIn's Awkward and Painful 'Getting Introduced' Request Form

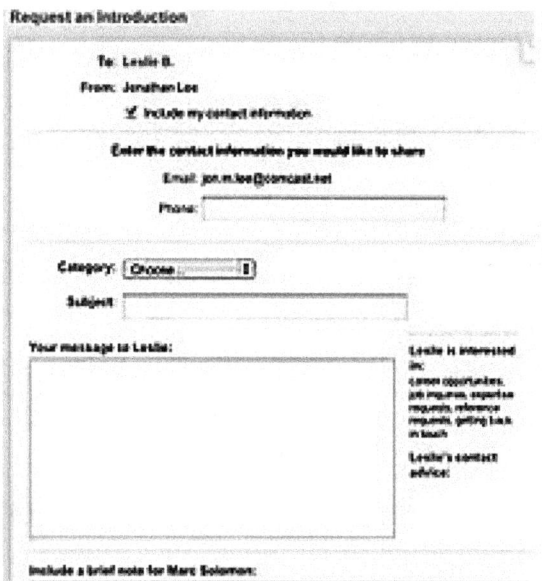

This is the way that LinkedIn implores a member to advance their networking opportunities through the intermediary – second person contact signifying the degree of separation between the member and the would-be contact.

His question is this: What happens ... how does this work?

> I hit send, a message goes to you. Do you only see my note to you - or the message to X (Leslie B. in this example) as well? And what about the person you know, who knows Leslie? How is that connection made? Automatically - or do you have to find the connection for me? Do they see my message to you, my message to Leslie?

The hypothetical scenarios go on for a few more paragraphs before the logic is tortured right out of the motivation for getting to the actual conversation stages – the linking out phase of the process. I appreciate these questions because they underscore the associative clunk factor of shuffling through an overloaded circuit of lateral connectors.

The community spirit of pay-it-forward reciprocity might work for random acts of kindness. But perhaps not so much for calculating and indiscriminate emails – especially from people we know more for their degree of separation than we do about them. Period.

The artifice of the social media back-scratch points to the exit ramp or the link-out. This is the realization that as gorgeous as that well-groomed garden is, all the growth happens within the narrow confines of Linkedin.com. It is a walled-in garden. That's why a thousand Facebook weeds makes more advertising perfume than the most painstaking bouquet of freshly cut resumes at LinkedIn.

We need to step on a few weeds, maybe even some poisonous ones, before any meaningful conversations can happen. That's where a nose for research meets an eye for opportunity and an ear for discussion. That kind of growth can only happen in soils and climates where the greatest variety of vegetation takes root.

The Cost of Free

While this resource is free, the vendor requests that we upload a listing of potential contacts from our own email directories that we can send invite to join LinkedIn. The benefit to us is that by expanding our network, we increase the size of the database. If we agree to sign-up we'll be able to search my network as well as those in your own who have already signed up with LinkedIn (or who you bring along).

There is also no requirement that you accept the invitation to join either. In the past, some may feel compromised or exposed for putting their credentials in the database. Some may have felt uncomfortable about asking their own contacts to consider joining.

These trepidations had died away by the teens decade of the 21st Century. In fact, any misgivings about surrendering private details have been overcome by social networks that promise an entire platform for hosting all varieties of virtual communications. The allure of viewing those carvings from the privacy of our imaginations is the trigger. And it works no matter what's hiding behind the password door.

Remember media bias? Think of that same partiality for attracting attention through social networks that a broadcast network can only dream about. The default setting for the platform version of Facebook is that social network-based information providers will swallow our personal histories whole for "posterity, police, and divorce lawyers." **(Gillmor, 2010)**[15]

It's up to the member to de-activate the archival function. Opt-in is set to the complete, if nakedly unabridged version. Facebook wants its members to spend the optimal spread of their waking hours on Facebook. Is this as sinister as it sounds? Or is a just reward for surrendering our personal privacy in exchange for citizenship in a virtual community?

The Downsides of Social Media

The most fundamental disconnect of current state web lies between our dual roles as content producers and consumers. It's one thing to shed aliases and handles as fluidly as we're pressed for passwords. It's quite another to be torn between our need for peer approval and self-protection. That's not a minor misalignment. That's a deep and impassable identity crisis. How the two are reconciled is not the next big app. It's the staging ground for the gathering storm perfection of...

- The rise of Facebook
- The fall of journalism
- The abyss of credibility

For the better half of two decades, we've been feeding the sociable media beast with friend affirmations. We want a sense of belonging, of inclusiveness. But if we pay for that community-building with back-scratches and platitudes that leaves a gaping hole between what we hope to be expressed and what we know to be true. It's not that Facebook praises are empty on arrival, but enforced by a culture of reciprocal transparency. As much as positive reinforcement is the elixir of choice for self-expression, it leaves us hungry for how others perceive us. It's tone deaf to the indifference of outsiders. Those are the potential employers who background check us out. But they're not looking for suitors, social circles, or listening to our echo chamber of megaphones.

They just want to know they can trust us and can't just take our word for it.

What would happen if none of us were allowed to post to our own social media profiles? Would our friends make up for the shortfall? Could our enemies commit *face crimes* and libel us with half-truths and fabrications? In a regulated web, non-vested observers would honor their own reputations by speaking to objectives, standards, and rankings — not how they've been blemished by greatness or influenced by the people they're profiling. Sounds like the ghost of journalistic myth-making? Sounds like a reason to pay for content in cash — not gratitude.

BUILD IT – AND THEY WILL DUMP

In the future, this darker Facebook would be compensated from both sides of the message exchange. Anonymous enemies would get to post unsubstantiated kiss-and-tells once they sign-up. Group members could pony up too. But they'd have to preempt these negative reviews with their own cathartic self-examinations. Posting enough of these face-saving gestures would earn enough credits to learn the actual identities of their blasphemers? No practicing journalist is in a competitive bargaining position in that business model.

The dark fantasy of an evil twin brother to Facebook may one day come to pass. It may inhabit a place once reserved for reporters who arbitrated once definable and containable questions like:

> *Can the public handle the truth about...?*

Facial truth may arrive without malevolent intentions. Some may even be noble in their naivete. For instance, it may be a libertarian impulse from Craigslist. If no one knows what breeds we kennel on the Internet, surely there's a universal understanding that flies under the longest of tails we wave. In the book of Craigslist, what people do in their uninhibited privacy is not only their own business but endows the publisher with the right of keeping their identities under the roof of one San Francisco-based Victorian.

This same Constitution that guarantees the right to free speech also protects the right to remain silent. Does that extend to the right to remain anonymous in our virtual identities?

It may be a social media partisan who believes that transparency, consensus, and may-the-best-idea win are all wrapped and sealed in the protective popularity of a Survey Monkey referendum. It most certainly is a loyal Wikipedia correspondent who adheres to the sacred tenets of Wikipedia editorial policies. Thou shalt do no original research (or synthesis of two or more existing ideas) in the unquestioning isolation of their passive voice and their hollow curiosity.

Can I Subtract You as My Enemy?

With those seeds in motion, would the particle-smashing collision that awaits this doubting world be that surprising? We would be spinning out of our social orbits by joining a site where...

- Alias predators post dubious half-truths
- These rumors require only a popular vote to become credible
- Such fabrications convince fence-sitters they're getting the whole story

How would we stop these allegations?

As Andrew Morris-Friedman speculates, the only way to lower the temperature without changing the subject is to post even more reprehensible stuff to attract even higher scores. In this dark counterweight to Facebook, one can't see their accusers unless they suffer the fools of self-effacement. That's how we actually identify our detractors in a world devoid of credibility – by being our own worst enemies.

What could be a more lucrative exercise in community damage control and shear predatory gawking? In such a fishbowl-like environment, partisans would queue for the chance to shape a fair and balanced view of our own profiles.

Approaching Would-be Contacts in a Social Network

Enough about dystopian social media scenarios. An important advantage to an investigator remains having a number of credible, reliable sources to depend on. Our existing social networks provides us with this. However, we should actively analyze our networks and work to expand them.

Consider that you are trying to get firsthand information about a target from a second party. By joining their social network, you move to infiltrating a professional network. From infiltration, you move to cultivation: Your goal is to find second-party sources with the exposure to be vested in an outcome (action). Self-preservation here is tempered with enough distance from the consequences to appear credible (observation).

We can see some of the limitations of looking to social networks as credible information sources. For now, let's shelve our research jerseys, and join the party in our dance outfits. *Putting yourself out there* is just the first step. We then move to infiltration – seeking a potential dance partner, ideally to glean first hand information from a second party.

When do we know we're dancing with flair and distinction? Those second party sources can speak, and do so, for first parties, i.e. employers. It's easier for most of us to start with a larger pool of potential teams or groups. We can then narrow down the individual members or those with specific skills, perspectives, prerogatives (like hiring us), or even the cachet of their own social networks.

Here are some helpful tips for reaching beyond our respective comfort zones and social circles.

Cultivating Contacts: Melting the Social Ice

Remember the last time you got spammed by a political party or special interest group? You might have felt taken down a notch in the social order. That's because there were probably many assumptions made in the communication that you didn't necessarily share or hold as priorities. Either way, direct marketing is a one-way conversation. That's not the goal of this exercise or of successful social networking. On the other hand, a few colorful teasers (like some current search projects for example) might be a good hook for luring the kind of attention and curiosity that would support a meaningful exchange.

Here's how that dynamic plays out in an active pursuit of new contacts:

1) **Try to focus on the ideal situation** *(not the perfect would-be contact)* – Instead of fixating on a particular individual, focus on groups that espouse a view we share, campaign we want to join, or even a firm or organization we want to work for. Consider eyewitnesses or first party members of a shared movement or interest.

2) **Play the outsider card** – Share with your contact what initially attracted you to them (from a distance). Because you are not yet acquaintances, you can speak with the candor and freshness that a close friend or confidant can't. Because you're a stranger, you speak for a very large and important group. Everyone your contact has yet to meet who share the premise from your original welcome email.

3) **Don't tell them your life story** – Keep the common ground you share to mutual experiences and/or contacts (people you both know in the same field). A long-winded introduction doesn't fly on email any more than it does in-person. I've also found that your gesture of reaching out is perceived with greater sincerity and receptivity when you're sharing something that happened to you, changed you, or inspired you to take action. It works in reverse when your patter becomes goal-oriented or future-directed.

4) Approach them as equals – No one likes to be seen as an object or an objective. Think of the last time you were *hit on* for money, personal favors, or the good of some self-interested group that would have otherwise ignored you if they hadn't jeopardized their own position. That's why most of us abhor the ultimate compromise – asking for things. It's in that compromised state where some of us equate the deep ancestral needs for companionship and sustenance to self-promotion and politicking. The truth is that you are horse-trading when you send a total stranger an invitation to join ranks. Playing the dance card is the reciprocal trading of networks through *connecting* or *friending*.

Don't Underestimate Your Own Worth

This is not a self-help book but...

As reinforcement for that last point, don't assume that the person you approach is assuming you're the question and they're the answer. Social networks can be excellent talent pools when you are trying to assemble an investigation team of diverse strengths and professional backgrounds. You may be knocking on someone else's door. That said, the door's likelier to open when the recipient can see how selling their own assets will form a mutual benefit.

It's easy when we're looking for employment to underplay our hands. We'll take a further look at this in **Unit Five** when we consider professional blogs as platforms for the domain expert we seek to interview. The long-term goal might be a string of consulting gigs or gainful employment. In the short-term? It's to convince our networking targets that they should be talking to you as much as you to them, no?

An interesting follow-up would be to play the academic card and talk with an established professional about the different aspects of an investigator's tool-set that you're covering in the course. A good opening line might be something like:

> *"In your own career what would be hardest to teach someone else without experiencing it directly?"*

> *"What are some of the skills you'd like to brush up on, or find out that could complement the core assets you bring to the table?"*

This is not a term paper assignment or a sales call. But I'm asking you to take the next step.

This request is based on the commitments you have already made by investing your time and effort in cultivating your own Knowledge-ABILITIES. It may not be apparent when we're knee-deep in query formations. The end-game here is not to become search whizzes but to let our research do the talking. Those are the talking points when we're opening up new doors and initiatives in the goals and objectives that inspired us to make these sacrifices in the first place. No website or Internet skill delivers that. It's ultimately up to us to get from searching to conversing.

Defining Boundaries and Failsafes

Just like the web that existed before social media, for every bullseye there are a thousand distractions that threaten to carry us past our original purpose and supporting objectives. That's why returning to the SPM ("Search Project Management") format is useful for grounding our network goals. It's focusing not just on people we'd like to meet but the specific interactions we're looking to conduct.

For starters, consider your SPM from both your target's perspective. Search targets are ruled by their own agendas and motivation vectors. The SPM is not a form of administration but an investigation's scope and boundaries — predetermined by objective measures (time, budget, goals). Here's an example of how that model shapes up in pursuing contacts within social media circles:

FIGURE 4.28: Applying SPM to Approaching Contacts in a Social Network

SPM step	Rationale	Positioning
Why: Purpose	Reason for the networking	You want to get paid twice a month, obtain affordable health insurance, have a place to go each day
What: Objectives and Expectations	Objectives are the supporting evidence Expectations anticipate available resources and likely constraints	You want to set up a series of informational interviews that may lead to opportunities not otherwise posted to job boards and company websites
How: Tools and Methods	Task and goal-based procedures	'Follow' contacts you aspire to meet but focus on the larger community of ideas, i.e. use your personal blog or page to showcase your research
When: Duration and Failsafes	Time commitment to search and noted failures to redirect project	You don't want to watch that kettle boil but you do want to track your overtures so you can drive the discussion if/when your targeted contacts circle back to you
Who: Offline follow-up	Who is a direct contact that will advance the goals of my project	Who, indeed? Informality is the operative goal here for getting new contacts to lower their guard, speak candidly, and provide instructive guidance

The mapping in Figure 4.28 does not imply that only contacts we actively pursue are the only ones worth pursuing, Many contacts happen serendipitously around less weightier conversation points than career goals. But a major benefit of social networks is often overlooked the moment we join them. Just because we want to be sociable doesn't means we put aside our research skills.

Let's leave jobs and potential income sources aside for a moment.

There are other goals achieved better through social networks than perhaps any other form of virtual communication. For example, investigators can create or develop a social network when we need to show the connections between the vested parties: suspect, victim, witnesses, legal counsel, etc.

As we'll do in **Unit Five**, even if we don't 'friend' a potential criminal, we can still map this type of network through the PCF and integrity vector models, and present it to clients. A social network shows the personal, first-party, authentic interactions between internal group members (family, interested friends) and external group members (law enforcement, public institutions, the media, etc.).

Social Network Assignment Checklist

Now that we have the format, how do we step through our networking paces with the full benefit of our Knowledge-ABILITIES? Here's one example checklist that I drafted for my students. This was the final assignment. However, the fruits of their social information efforts were intended to be timeless and self-sustaining. Long after any could recall their final grades, the lasting benefit is in the informed schmoozing practiced by all consummate networkers:

1) *Join a social network. Determine a network and engagement strategy based on interview candidates you are considering from your background research.*

2) *Conduct interviews and searches for last class. Apply the lessons of perspective-taking to your candidate interviews and to the nature of the questioning done while conducting the primary information-gathering.*

3) *Determine what elements of your own career portfolio to publish on your page or blog.*

4) *Send invitations out to active contacts and extended community.*

5) *Select and perform one of these assignment options:*

    a) *Look-up three potential contacts within an organization who will help you secure employment within that organization. Conduct background research on all three.*

    b) *Reference experts in three different professions related to your ongoing investigation. Assess their credentials and their own professional networks, using the factors and metrics you learned in* **Units Three** *and* **Four**.

    c) *Bring the results of these activities to class.*

6) *Include background research and alerts/notifications.*

Now let's organize those steps, using SPM:

FIGURE 4.29: Applying SPM to the Social Network Assignment Checklist

SPM step	Rationale	Positioning
Why: Purpose	Reason for the networking	You want to have meaningful exchanges with influential contacts whose whose reputations precede them (networking targets)
What: Objectives and Expectations	Objectives are the supporting evidence Expectations anticipate available resources and likely constraints	Demonstrate your use of query formation in **Unit Two** (syntax, semantics, operators...) by using a commercial search engine to locate affiliated members within your network and theirs Use this same approach to highlight special skills or unique insights that will help you advance goals addressed in your search target's work and expertise
How: Tools and Methods	Task and goal-based procedures	Use a search engine other than Google or Bing that helps to connect this goal of yours with your networking targets SUGGESTION: Social bookmarking sites like Delicious are helpful for finding specialized search engines that focus on your area of interest
When: Duration and Failsafes	Time commitment to search and noted failures to redirect project	Use your research to write an email that will trigger a positive response from your search target. It's up to you if you follow through, then drop it (and don't wait out Twitter for the next tweet to land!)
Who: Offline follow-up	Who is a direct contact that will advance the goals of my project	It's always a bonus to pick folks who are within driving range for that follow-up coffee or the chance to intercept at speaking engagements

SEARCH TO CONVERSE

We create or develop social networks when we need to show the relationships and connections between the vested parties. One example is in a case: suspect, victim, witnesses, law enforcement, etc. We can map this type of network through models like PCF and SPM and present it to our clients.

In such a mapping, a social network shows the personal, first party, authentic interactions between internal group members (family, close friends/advisers...) and external group members.

Search to Converse ("STC") is the orientation for honing our investigations. It means that the main purpose of our search projects is not to amass as much evidence as possible. It's to collect just enough to make it actionable – not collecting for its own sake.

STC involves mapping our evidence to the purpose and objective of the investigation. It includes the following elements and activities:

1. Alerts and notifications
2. Daily progress on blogs
3. Joining professional networks and cultivating contacts
4. Assessing social networks and public record searches

> *Definition: Search to Converse ("STC")*
>
> *A brief but compelling model for prior research on individuals that should be engaged directly to corroborate, dispute, and augment the evidence in question.*

Putting Networks in Play

Diagrams have their merits. They're visual and help us to work and document our work in an organized and systematic way. But the real pay-off is not filling in a bunch of boxes but engaging in the discussions that happen outside those boxes. How do we connect our research approach with an immediate and tangible goal, one that demonstrates the common ground we share with our potential networking targets?

So what did my students do? They found folks in each of their networks (LinkedIn, Twitter, Facebook, Instagram...) that work in their chosen field (professional investigations). Students then emailed and asked them to comment about their professional roles and how they assumed those roles.

Sometimes those emails can read as scripted, a little stiff. For instance, you're being too formal if a personal introduction reads like a cover letter for employment. Envision the fulfilling of your objective before trading war stories, cultivating contacts, or developing an expertise around collection agency operations. That's how you connect your background and education to the topics you showcase in your research practice – those bloggable topics where you seek to...

- Distinguish your expertise and be a beacon for best practices,
- Package a set of services unique to your offering, and
- Make the biggest impact in your own right.

The biggest redirect I give them is to broaden their focus – starting with the larger target like a group or organization first. Then we're narrowing down to a particular person because of their connections, accomplishments, shared interests, expertise, etc. Whatever draws you to that person is the *what* or objectives section of your search log.

UNIT FOUR: Sense-making Through Information Context | Page 4:75

Sound right to your ears?

Hurdles persist in the searching to conversing transition. Yes, these overtures connect to each student's own background. Yes, the intention is to bridge their prior experience to their new set of skills (or renewed appreciation of skills they had all along). However, that's no guarantee of an explicit connection between our networking goals and the current passions and/or positions of the networking target.

Don't hear back from your targets? The next time out, I recommend:

1. Toning down the deafening ambition trapped in your brain, and
2. Letting that ambition fuel the determination to rebuild the original grounds for a meeting.

Remember, this appointment is prefaced on a shared bond such as a vested interest, belonging to a common group, or unified by a shared goal. Presenting those agenda-setting bonds can lead to a rich exchange of views, contacts, job leads, etc. Often that extra distance means stepping back, not drilling down. For instance, one smart approach is the added perspective of working in multiple fields you share with your targets, not a single-minded pursuit of an unwavering goal.

Careful here. There is a risk of fixating too much on single individuals to the detriment of our larger networking goals. As we saw earlier in **Unit Four**, the referral requests on LinkedIn are clunky at best and invasive when the pursuit is through third or fourth degrees of separation. It's usually more productive to break through directly by using some of the query formation techniques and people finder tools we introduced in **Unit Three**.

Another approach is to contact alumni from the same academic programs. Seeking out contacts who document a career shift *after* completion of the program is a great way to substantiate their use of the same credential you're now pursuing as well.

When searching to conversing goes smoothly, it's rarely an effortless undertaking. Documentation manages to be exhaustive and airtight. There is not a single wasted description or idle observation. Overtures to targets is honest, compelling, fact-based, provocative – and completely worthy of a response. It's always a sensitive issue when we ask directly for professional guidance from an unknown actor. But this is no cold call. A consummate networker can diffuse the awkwardness. Referencing your relative distance from the field you're trying to crack is an invitation for perspective-gathering and engagement.

Determining Your Digital Identity

> *"We wouldn't worry so much about what people thought of us if we knew how seldom they did."*
>
> – Samuel Johnson

In **Unit Two,** we first explored the Query Formation equivalence for googling the babysitter. We used semantics to determine if I was in fact 'the Marc Solomon' – star of Internet research stage and screen. We further qualified my birth name with a list of possible area codes within the Boston Massachusetts metropolitan area:

> *"Marc Solomon" (617 OR 978 OR 508 OR 781) boston*

In **Unit Three**, we reviewed some common people finder tools for making accurate IDs, conducting background checks, and gathering contact information. We also considered tools that document the assets and properties of our potential search targets.

Now that we're beyond the mechanics of query building, we're at the point where it's actually getting personal: What is the difference between our Google profiles and our actual background and credentials? Or as someone who may have had vengeance in their hearts, and used a Facebook page for their catharsis...

- ■ What are some of the distortions and where in the self-reporting do you see the compromises?
- ■ Which of those pieces in our checkered pasts are better documented than others?

Perhaps, applying PCF is the best way to begin this deconstruction:

> *What would you like to change about what a third person rendering of you would look like?*

Passing through our own *looking glasses* may be advised here. And it's not navel-gazing or a walk on the wild side in pursuit of some low impact aerobics. Let's say we might one day wish to achieve some rather conventional life goals like marriage, family, and career success? In that light, we squint into the glare of violence, sex, and any inferences of criminal behavior under the lens of our digital identities. Questioning what we see *is* the point. We look into this mirror with the humility that we would extend the same unassuming hand of fair play and neutrality to the digital identities of our search targets.

To paraphrase Samuel Johnson, human vanity is a blindspot so large, we could fit love, ambition, and jealousy within its shadowing borders, and still have room for all our Facebook albums. There is no piety or superiority in stating the simple matter of fact that we all come to live in glass houses. The true test isn't how well we see through the glass. It's how well we hold ourselves up to the same judgments we make about those landing above our own personal radars.

Alerts and Notifications

In her book *Information Trapping: Real-Time Research on the Web*, Tara Calishain makes researching more efficient for the thousands of academics, journalists, scientists, and professionals for whom the Web is an indispensable tool – as well as bloggers, genealogists, and other hobbyists with a passion to pursue. She does so by teaching the latest techniques in creating ongoing information-gathering systems that are as automated as possible. Instead of the usual static, single instance of finding information, Calishain demonstrates how to use RSS feeds, page monitoring tools, and other software so readers can move from browsing to setting information traps.

These will notify you of changes to local communities and to individual websites.

FIGURE 4.30: Example of an Alerts and Notifications Interface

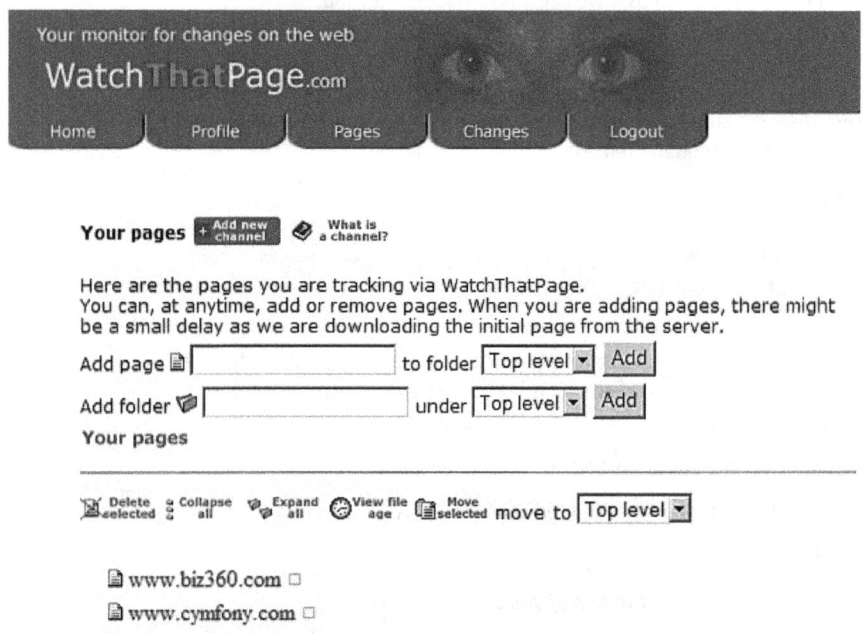

Watch that Page is an alerting service that notifies subscribers of changes to root domains and subdomains in a website of interest. This tool can be helpful on normally static company sites when a change in management or a particular alliance or product line is anticipated.

<u>Tips for Searching Social Media Profiles</u>

As we discussed in our introduction to the Deep and Invisible Web in **Unit Three,** it can be quite difficult to nail down fluid or continually evolving web pages, a.k.a. dynamic content. How do we know if we're trying to capture the proverbial lightening in a bottle? That's when the page in our browser ends with the following characters:

1. ?
2. %
3. +
4. $
5. cgi-bin

These pages could be flash demos, pop-ups or i-frames. In lay terms, this could be an ad that requires a cookie to generate or a travel reservation that only lasts for a specific duration. Without a static URL, the page cannot be tagged or regenerated without starting at the specific root site or database.

Fortunately, most digital credentialing is easier to pin down. In effect, the regular query formation rules apply. That means a combination of syntax and semantics can help generate lists of potential employees, experts, customers, or like-minded colleagues based on interest, location, experience, and any number of demographic qualifiers.

For example, one difference on Facebook between finding a potential date or new hire means means searching for 'women' in concert with 'diversity' in tandem with the sourcing 'location.' Those additional qualifications change the intention from a pick-up line to a prospect call. In terms of outputs, it helps to apply the information type filtering we learned in **Unit Two**. For instance, some social networks include such default fields as geography, employer, and alma mater as default outputs for their in-depth results. Sometimes those options change depending on network or our status within them.

If our major objective is name generation, we might not even bother with search pages. Lots of people are often highlighted as listings in directories contained within single PDF documents. Again, our ability to anticipate format types is key for informing the most most productive social media searches. Also, it sounds strange, but sometimes a straight forward professional search can become ensnared by the habits and preferences of SEO campaigns that distort your earnest intent. For instance, a search on 'nurse jobs' can turn racy with little qualification, or imagination for that matter.

FIGURE 4.31: Using Syntax and Semantics to Elevate Desired Working Terms in a Field of Choice

```
site:linkedin.com "knowledge management" relo package inurl:~job
```
About 97 results (0.36 seconds)

▶ Haak
I started my sales & marketing **career** in the Netherlands where I was responsible for .... cost of the proposed **relocation package** to the hiring executive. ...
www.linkedin.com/pub/dir/+/Haak - Cached

Associate Manager, Internal Communications at Blizzard ...
Nov 18, 2010 ... Location: Velizy (southwest of Paris) - a **relocation package** will be ...
Experience of **knowledge management** and / or business analysis ...
www.linkedin.com/**jobs**?viewJob=&jobId... - Cached

Sue anne
Title: **Recruitment** Sourcing Specialist at Research In Motion ... Manager - Channel Marketing, Indonesia (based in Indonesia) **Relocation package** will be considered. .... Title: EMEA **Knowledge Management**; Demographic info: Amsterdam Area, ...
www.linkedin.com/pub/dir/Sue+anne/+ - Cached

Lisa Blackmon | LinkedIn
Negotiated approximately 50 **salary** offers and dozens of sign-on bonuses/**relocation packages** annually at both ... The Braintrust: **Knowledge Management** Group ...
www.linkedin.com/pub/lisa-blackmon/08/B20/741 - Cached

Deepti Gudup - Project Manager at TechMahindra | LinkedIn
The Hague Area, Netherlands - Project Manager at TechMahindra
o Implementation of **work package** and Delivery closure formalities o **Knowledge Management** and transition to maintenance teams .... Jointly developed the web application to assist **relocation** of resources (employees and hardware assets) to ...
nl.linkedin.com/in/deeptigudup - Netherlands - Cached

Scott Gavin profiles | LinkedIn
Title: Expatriate **Recruitment** & **Relocation** Representative at Aramco ... current **jobs** or the **employment package**- contact me via LinkedIn or visit our NEW ...
www.linkedin.com/pub/dir/Scott/Gavin - Cached

SHUM
Senior Manager - Channel Marketing, Indonesia (based in Indonesia) **Relocation package** will be considered. If interested, kindly drop me an email at ...
www.linkedin.com/pub/dir/+/SHUM - Cached

Google Query in 2010. Note that keyword highlighting is in effect, even for term expansion phrases related to 'relo.'

FIGURE 4.32: The Changing Face of Using Search Engines to Network

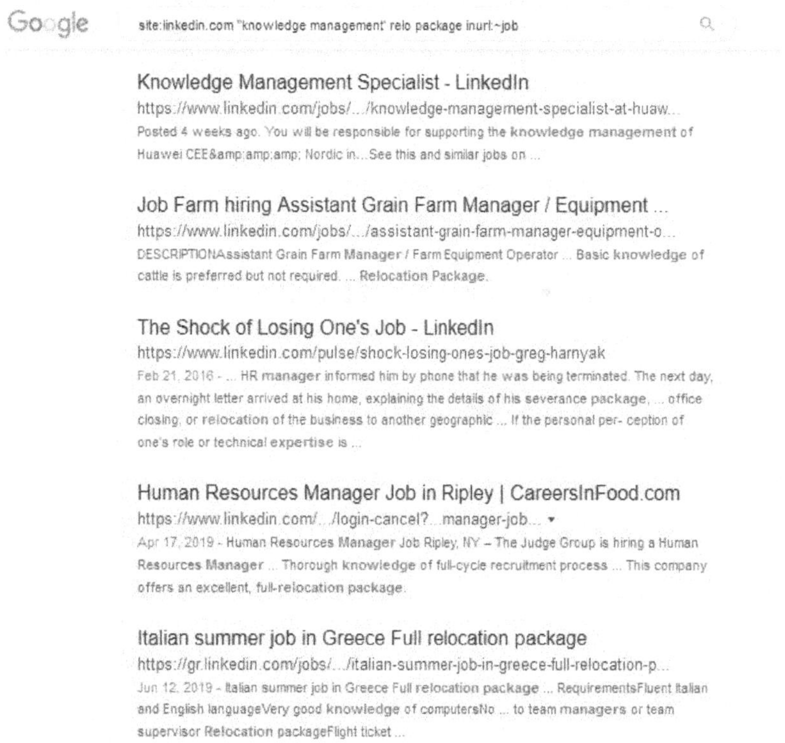

Google   site:linkedin.com "knowledge management" relo package inurl:~job

Knowledge Management Specialist - LinkedIn
https://www.linkedin.com/jobs/.../knowledge-management-specialist-at-huaw...
Posted 4 weeks ago. You will be responsible for supporting the knowledge management of Huawei CEE&amp; Nordic in...See this and similar jobs on ...

Job Farm hiring Assistant Grain Farm Manager / Equipment ...
https://www.linkedin.com/jobs/.../assistant-grain-farm-manager-equipment-o...
DESCRIPTIONAssistant Grain Farm Manager / Farm Equipment Operator ... Basic knowledge of cattle is preferred but not required. ... Relocation Package.

The Shock of Losing One's Job - LinkedIn
https://www.linkedin.com/pulse/shock-losing-ones-job-greg-harnyak
Feb 21, 2016 - ... HR manager informed him by phone that he was being terminated. The next day, an overnight letter arrived at his home, explaining the details of his severance package, ... office closing, or relocation of the business to another geographic ... If the personal per- ception of one's role or technical expertise is ...

Human Resources Manager Job in Ripley | CareersInFood.com
https://www.linkedin.com/.../login-cancel?...manager-job... ▼
Apr 17, 2019 - Human Resources Manager Job Ripley, NY – The Judge Group is hiring a Human Resources Manager ... Thorough knowledge of full-cycle recruitment process ... This company offers an excellent, full-relocation package.

Italian summer job in Greece Full relocation package
https://gr.linkedin.com/jobs/.../italian-summer-job-in-greece-full-relocation-p...
Jun 12, 2019 - Italian summer job in Greece Full relocation package ... RequirementsFluent Italian and English languageVery good knowledge of computersNo ... to team managers or team supervisor Relocation packageFlight ticket ...

Here's the same query in 2019. Where are all the job candidates? Where are all the people? Where's the bleeping hit count?

SOCIAL BOOKMARKING: SOMEBODY KNOWS THE SITES I'VE SEEN

Unlike a professional networking site, a tagging or social bookmarking tool is focused less on finding people and more on discovering or recovering a useful site. Tagging is a productive and self-referential way to unify all the search experiences worth repeating.

Have you ever created a favorites placeholder in your web browser? Have you ever saved several if not dozens of bookmarks to record a visit to a page to which one day you might return (and never do?)

Can I ask you something?

How often do you even think of returning? If the answer is infrequently at best you're not alone. But if you think your isolation must persist, then you may find yourself alone fairly soon.

Drum roll please for social bookmarking.

I'll be honest. In some of my past classes the technology part of teaching Internet Research was a real hardship for some folks. You might have heard of the distinction between *digital immigrants* and *natives* to describe: (1) those of us who grew up with the web as a fact of life and, (2) those of us who are astounded every time we login. **(Prensky, 2001)**[16] The student I'm describing wasn't an immigrant but a digital *deportee*. They needed research to be tangible, linear, and fixed in one place. Virtual was not part of their dress code.

Core Social Media Technologies

Clearly, this factor is not in play with your sizable investment in making information useful. So here we go. I will be introducing you to three web technologies for documenting and presenting web-based investigations through social media — some of which you may already be practicing and observing:

> **1) Social Bookmarking:** Fulfilling the promise of no memorization. Everything's activated when you need it.
>
> **2) RSS Readers:** Realizing the need to boil the internet ocean down to a pond. Where the fish are plenty and they bite back.
>
> **3) Blogs:** Your true calling put up in Internet lights for all to see. Especially the folks you want to converse with on future projects.

The one enduring benefit common to all three is the confidence that the roles they perform are not short-term or prone to becoming marginalized by the next big thing. That's because they can do something that's lost on trendsetters. They can't grasp the value in their sexy, top dollar devices because these technologies are about making information work for you.

The true power lies not in upgrading to the latest and greatest but managing our projects and attentions according to our own interests and priorities. That's what social bookmark sites (a.k.a. tagging engines), RSS Readers, and blogging platforms do for us — make information work for us and not the other way around.

The Benefits of Social Tagging

It's easier to show than it is to tell.

Yes, there are benefits for knowledge capture. We can recover not only pages worth revisiting but even the query language from instructive searches that led us there in the first place. But the biggest benefit is the network effect. That's the serendipitous spark that ignites when our crowdsourcing colleagues take the pain and effort to describe an experience worth repeating.

For us investigators, that's the very definition of search success. The key to repeating that success is to recall the paths we take to get from questions to answers. Each tag is a breadcrumb that jogs our memory for particular sources and/or searches that will help build on that knowledge (or avoid a past pitfall). This helps settle immediate scores and may well continue forward on future search expeditions.

Social bookmarking is a way of saving these places on a dedicated webpage that you control. Better yet, the upkeep is no more challenging than clicking an icon when a site worth saving passes through. If you care about your own time and managing your Internet-based research, then tagging is a big deal.

Tag Clouds

Before we get grounded in the practice of tagging as a daily practice, let's wander a bit in the tag cloud to understand some of the key distinctions and benefits.

FIGURE 4.33: Defining Tag Clouds

Social Bookmarking
Tag Cloud

- Your own wiring
- Network effects
- Tagging engine

This kind of indexing has long been the work of information scientists, taxonomists, and catalogers that adhere to the traditions of the disciplines they classify. In social bookmarking there are no such conventions – only the top-of-mind association that legions of searchers summon when they're looking to affirm the authority and 'aboutness' of a potential source of their investigations.

Let's look more closely at what goes into tag clouds and why this is a huge productivity gain for the **Knowledge-ABLED**:

1) **Your Own Wiring** – Tagging enables you to recall productive sites and even search sessions according to the way you recall things. For instance, let's say you're tagging a database that yields some successful clinical trials for a rare disease that's anything but rare in your family. You will literally *save* that success according to the patient's name or referring doctor, or whatever detail is likeliest to conjure up your discovery process. That's the learning sequence you will not to revisit at a later stage of the trial, disease, and investigation.

2) **Network Effects** – Tagging your work to a dedicated tagging site has the added benefit of leveraging the tags that have already been referenced by other registrants on the site. That means you can generate a listing of sites already tagged as well as the popularity of the site itself. A high number of tagging counts is an important validation that the source is frequently cited and/or productive in the investigations of others.

3) **Tagging Engine** – The other important connection with tagging is that dedicated tagging sites organize the web around the respective vocabularies of every tagger who joins their network. Thus we can save terms to the words that we invoke to summon connections. But what about all the other terms that would never occur to us? Leveraging tagging sites as search engines produces high value results lists of potential resources, but also a richer yield of tags that are also relevant to our research.

FIGURE 4.34: The Network Effects Benefits of Social Bookmarking

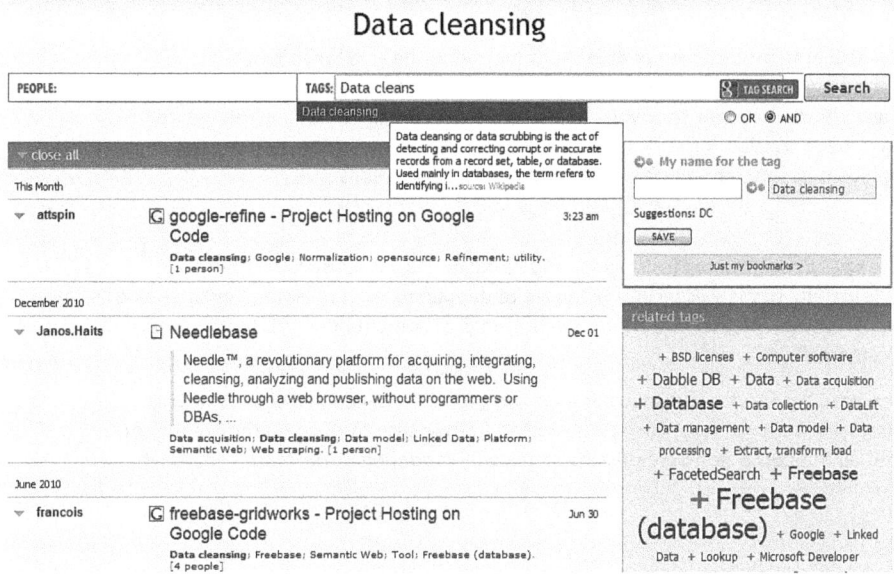

Social bookmarking helps us leverage the communal aspects of pooling resources together – certainly an improvement on the static nature of a favorites folder, as we see above in a tagging engine called Faviki, we can even summon on-the-fly definitions for the terms we're using in our tags.

The Limitations of Keeping Our Bookmarks Under Wraps

Bookmarking or what Microsoft refers to as a "Favorites Folder" is a traditional if somewhat static and inflexible way to store a list of websites worth remembering.

But there is no way to annotate these sites according to the experience they represent. Even though we've created a placeholder for archiving important discoveries, we can't reconnect them to our discovery process.

For instance, let's say that a database comprising the insurance records of physicians in Massachusetts were to be listed under health-related bookmarks. What if that site was also instructive as a tool for looking into malpractice claims on a doctor you're investigating?

This context introduces other dimensions that may be well worth exploring but obscured by the linear and cumbersome way that bookmarks are stored. In this illustration, the terms 'Malpractice' can be tagged. So can 'investigation' or 'Medical Errors' or any other noun or predicate that inspires us to remember the context for applying the bodies of knowledge documented in these resources. For the record, this documentation dynamic was begun in 2003 by the now dormant Del.icio.us. In its day, Del.icio.us was a magnet for leverage-worthy research links.

Additional Tagging Tips

1) Key words or noun phrases?

One distinction that is rarely addressed is that when we talk about key words we assume this includes compound words or multiple terms, a.k.a. phrases. For example, the American Dialect Society routinely includes hyphenates like 'game-changer' and 'shovel-ready' as nominations for its word of the year. Phrases referring to past political scandals or pronouncements like 'Zombie bank' or 'Smart power' are also fair game. **(Zimmer, 2009[17])**.

While this practice works fine in deliberations between people the same cannot be said for software programming. Just as nature abhors a vacuum, search engines despise the blank characters between words. Most social tagging sites treat any phrase broken with a white space as a separate tag. Other engines create lookup tables that match the tags we're considering with those already indexed. Some invite us to separate our tags with delimiters that treat phrases as separate terms such as commas or semi-colons.

2) One or many?

One thing we don't have to do is save a separate tag for singular and plural nouns, i.e. 'prison' and 'prisons.' Another is to use vague or overly general terms – especially when we're deepening our understanding of unique aspects of that topic, i.e. 'crime.' I recommend that you create single strings of compound words to differentiate the categories that are likely to emerge.

For instance, if we do a Delicious search on crime and entertainment we get a site tagged by 2000+ members called "Global Incident Map Displaying Terrorist Acts, Suspicious Activity." If we click through on the number of taggers, we'll see a full sweep for all the tags used to identify the site, a GPS rendering of Hazardous Material 'Situations and Incidents.'

The result is that we can create more purposeful headings like...

- CrimeMaps
- CrimeRetail
- CrimePredictions and so on...

Why no space between the terms? As we see below, if you use phrases in our tags then the tagging engines will list each term separately as its own tag. Not cool!

However, the engine will save as one tag if you create compound words from these noun phrases or add placeholders between terms:

```
SearchEnginesearch_enginesearch+engine
```

3) One or many?

Here's an important caveat about the pages you bookmark. They are bound to change no matter how thoroughly we document their temporary existence. News articles, calendar listings, or even transactional details like airline reservations are highly fluid, and resistant to any kind of placeholder. One workaround is to bookmark the cache result that is stored in the search index long after the same record is taken off the production server:

1. A referring link is broken now that the article has been removed...
2. However, the cache link of the same URL captures the removed article and is now taggable on a number of news sites that carried the same story

4) Drop anchor — tag away!

Finally, register with a tagging site like Digg, Reddit, StumbleUpon, or Diigo. Next, start tagging away on anything worth repeating. That includes webpages with explanations such as search engines with special features. It also includes the actual queries we create with semantic patterns and syntactic strings worth leveraging again. That means we're saving the roadmaps, not just the destination sites.

FIGURE 4.35: Saving Journeys – not just Destinations

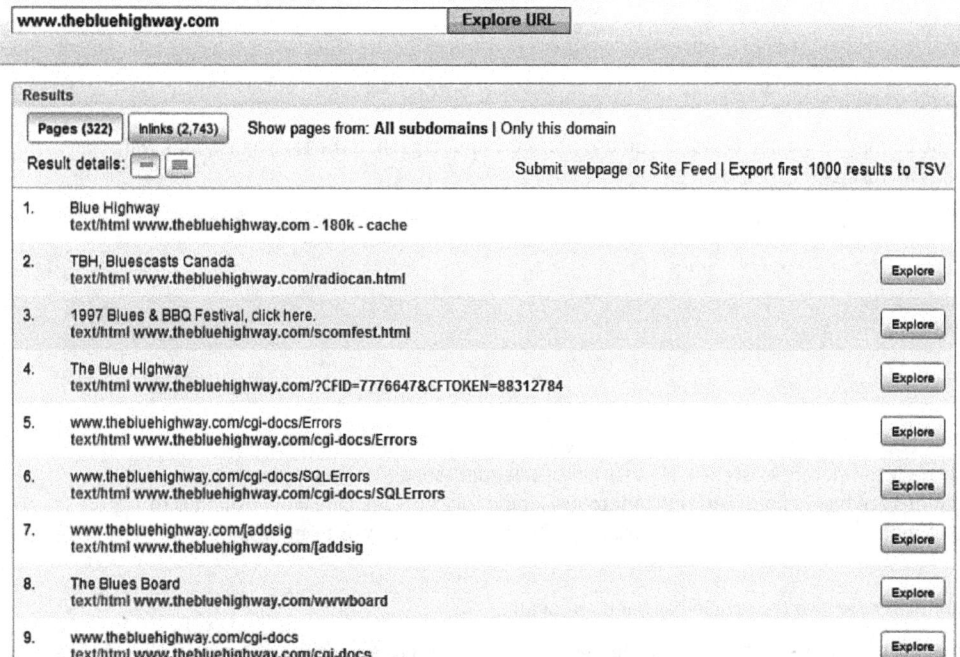

These examples of semantic searches are illustrations of success. Each one holds the particular tweaks for moving us from our original SPM objectives to 'how' we get at the evidence we're using to support our original purpose. Just a few more tweaks and we can apply the same queries to entirely new search projects.

See? It's not a wild leap from **Unit Two** to the socially-enabled sharing of endorsed content through tagging engines. Your hits should be smaller in number and higher quality than what you might expect with the bigtime engines. The reason is that Google is supply-driven. Everyone who covets 15 minutes of fame or a higher placement in its PageRank is concocting Google potions. That's the essence of commercial search. Tagging engines, however, are demand-driven. And that's music to the ears of most researchers. Any *hit* in a tagging engine search is a positive response – not a plea. And the response is ... hey, this is a repeatable experience.

At the risk of boring you I'll say it again: if it bears repeating, it's worth tagging.

SECTION 4:4 | Misinformation as an Information Source —
Misinformation: When Context Disappears

So far **Unit Four** has been about the perspective-gathering that we need for our research. This happens when our spyglasses focus in on (1) human affairs, and (2) why people do what they do. Modeling the motives of information providers is a decisive action for us observers. Piety is not commanding us to sit in the judgment of others. A healthy skepticism requires that we don't take one provider's perspective as the final, definitive word. Frameworks like PCF and the Vectors of Integrity are measurement tools towards that end. They gauge the distance between words and deeds: The universal metric for determining the level of attention (and often belief) we invest as message recipients.

Knowing the context doesn't just mean we can decide for ourselves. It gets us beyond the immediate *eye of the beholder*. It enhances what neuro-scientists refer to as 'theory of mind.' This concept addresses our ability to understand that others have beliefs, desires and intentions that are different from our own. **(Premack, Woodruff, 1978)**[18] It means we can see clear through the single-minded purpose of providers to the processing of those messages. We can assess how the layerings of meanings are sorted through, saved, discarded, and integrated into our existing world views, memories, and appetites for detail.

> *Definition: Theory of Mind*
>
> *The perspective-gathering that enables us to understand the priority scales, trust systems, and expectations that govern the everyday conduct of the individuals and group behaviors which we need to rationalize as researchers.*

But what happens when the force of a message is so great, it overpowers our reasoning? It overwhelms our ability to think critically. We can't anticipate. We can't process. We can only react. If it sounds like we've suddenly gone from dispassionate investigators to embroiled victims. That's not a trick of the light. That's the disarming nature of character assassinations: The demonizing of individuals and groups that stand in the way of the misinformation provider.

THE LIMITED PERSPECTIVES OF INFORMATION PROVIDERS

We now shift from the expansive context of recipients back to the more limited perspectives of providers.

Have you ever been on a call with someone you don't know? Have you ever been anxious about whose turn it was to speak first? Chances are, if the stranger called the meeting, you're not that concerned. You expect to be on the receiving end. Information providers are presenters and facilitators. Providers are on speaker. Information recipients are on mute.

Naturally, we all have a hand in both camps. It didn't take the advent of social media to blur the boundaries between content producers and consumers. The art of conversation is largely a study in switching off between both roles. But when that exchange happens in a set of search results and web pages, the conversation is strained and the information flows in one direction. This more traditional call and response pattern is similar to the economic model of supply and demand.

When we are providers, at least in more formal and binding communication channels, it's hard to escape this timeless and cautionary dictum:

> "Once it's out there, you can't take it back."

That's a recurrent question in our minds as individuals and as group members. Our communications are now recorded. From the most prolific political speech to the most casual off-handed tweet. Dialogs, monologues, blogs, search logs, and keystrokes of mental fogs: There's a digital recollection of what we've done with words and numbers.

However, that reminder for discretion may not lead to the reworking or even self-sensoring of material that finds its voice in forums, many extending well beyond the initial context. Anyone who's ever had an email of theirs forwarded to unknown individuals, knows this disorientation firsthand. The message goes out to others they either don't know or care to involve. That's when we grasp that loss of control: The realization that the follow-up interpretation may be quite removed from the original intention.

Now amplify the loss of context by the number of our followers, collaborators, and peers plugged into the same email servers that we are. That's a boat load of garbled communications, misinterpreted intentions, and unforeseen outcomes. Is my conclusion that public pronouncements and even private peer communications need to be better vetted? Say, the same way news articles were proofed by copy editors?

No, not because more attentive proofing isn't a good thing. It's not because *thinking,* even twice — before we *send* isn't a sound policy. It's because this is a book for researchers, not communicators. That's what we investigators must keep in mind as we begin to unpack passive, edgy, and downright hostile sources of misinformation, even intimidation. First and foremost in our thinking is that...

- ■ Only the most thoughtful and deliberate providers actually think through the implications of what they communicate
- ■ The clearer the motive for communicating, the less likely the information provider we're sourcing falls into this camp

Let me explain.

We talk about opportunities when we use information. We think in terms of risk when others do so. No risk assessment performed by an internet researcher is complete without considering misinformation – the unfounded hearsay that passes judgment as quickly as it spreads. So how do we pass better judgment and substantiate the information we pass onto our own peers, and clients, and networks?

The key to being Knowledge-ABLED is to steal a page from the PCF and Vectors of Integrity. We reapply the same principles used earlier to assess message recipients. Now we leverage them to weigh the merits of our sources. We can sort out what they're saying through three perspectives:

1. **Authenticity** – How directly an information source participates in the facts and opinions they produce.

2. **Credibility** – The difference between how a group describes itself and is depicted by others.

3. **Conjugation** – The distinction between interpersonal and group communications: How that impacts what, when, and to who digital information is communicated.

Don't Just Take My Word for it

Remember back in **Unit One** when we first broached the subject of blindspots? Rather than specific weaknesses, our blindness is rooted in our own oblivion. They may be personal shortcomings. They may be imperfections, or quirks that we choose to ignore. Either way, we are not the best communicators of our own impaired perceptions.

This design flaw is of particular note to information providers in the age of social media, especially in a medium that based on first person referrals to one's self. This is not narcissism or self-centeredness. These are the new rules of the game – the shared understandings between providers and recipients:

1. The first understanding is that I'm providing you with information about me.

2. The second less understood assumption is that I may not be the most qualified person to do this.

Once again, we're up against the integrity vector that spans from authenticity on one end to credibility at the opposite extreme. Can you trust me? Perhaps not. But understanding the inherent flaws of first persons and parties as the subject of their own messages increases confidence in our own Knowledge-ABILITIES.

FIGURE 4.36: Tracing the Source Origins of Information Providers Through Link Analysis

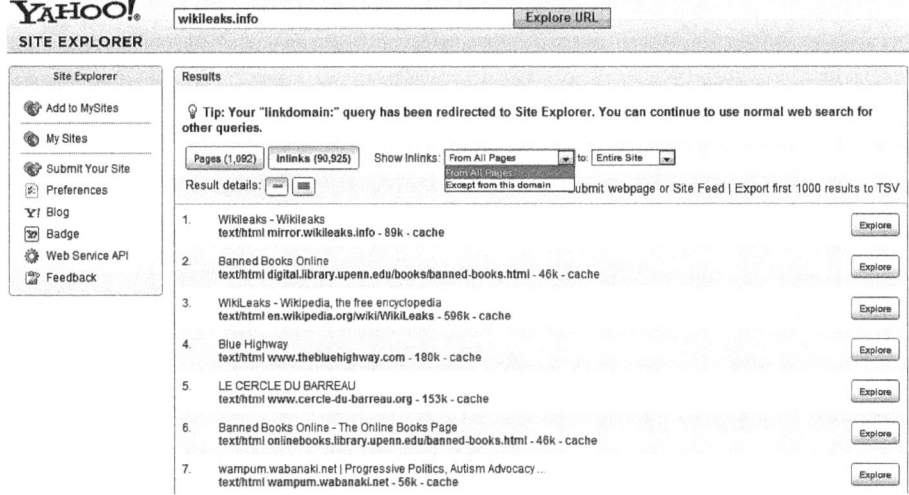

The linkdomain syntax lists all web pages that include hyperlinks to the target site root "wikileaks.info."

FIGURE 4.37: Focusing on One Prolific Linker to the Target Information Provider

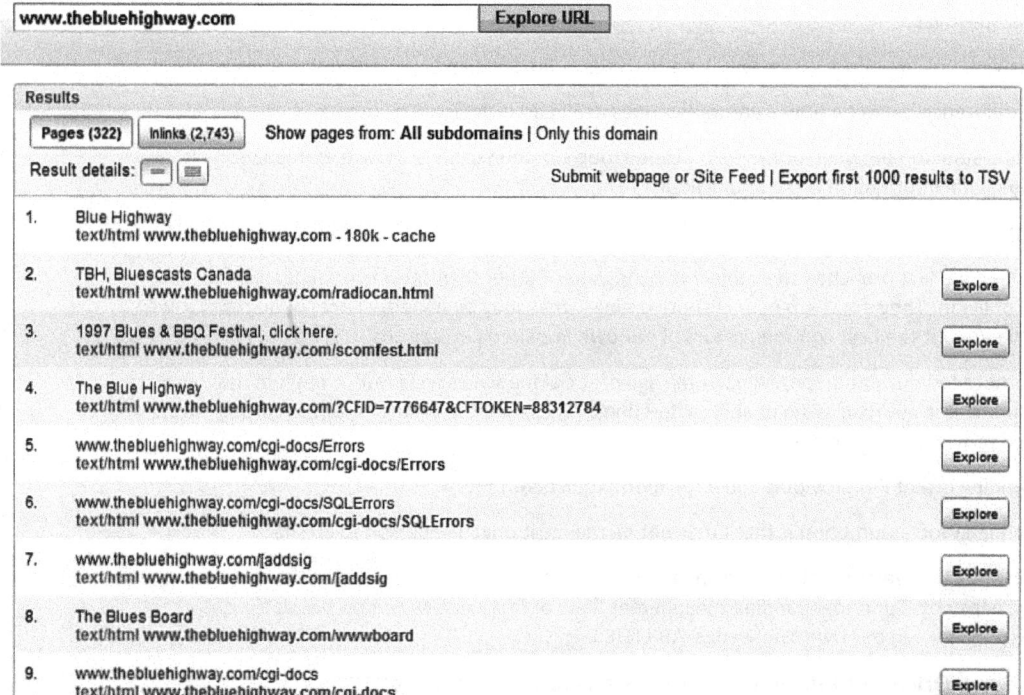

This screen capture illustrates the deepest of the most – the 322 individual webpages from the same site root (domain) that references the original search target (WikiLeaks.info). Link analysis like that performed here enables us to see not only referring links but the kinds of references our information providers cultivate to support their cases or even sell their products.

Going Negative

An old college friend of mine and I were watching one of our grainy college videos from the early 1980s. One production consisted mostly of off-air ads from the early 80s set to a David Byrne/Brian Eno-like avant guard collaboration. We were both taken with a fast food commercial where to pre-pubescent girls rode their bikes into town for an unstructured outing at the local McDonald's.[19] Chugging fries 'n cokes without a cellphone?

Imagine the consternation of letting a nine-year-old out on their own to experience retail commerce, moving traffic and total strangers? What parent 21st Century parental figure could ever live down the decision to let their own kids grow-up?

The other aspect of defensive behavior that's fascinating is the notion that people take these precautions for assertive or *control purposes*. It's easy to regard this aspect of human nature as an ingrained suspicion or pervasive social distrust. Perhaps. But I think it boils down to the fact that in the scarcity culture, most people feel more control over preventing sneak attacks than enabling a pleasant surprise. In the external world, negative information is processed much more quickly than positive news. It's the original homeland defense.

After my undergraduate video days, I moved into a post-grad political consulting program where we were taught that playing to peoples' fears was neither inherently evil nor virtuous. It depended on two factors:

1. Your candidate's base or loyalists will remain steadfast in their support.
2. The alienations you seed reverberate in the fears and doubts in what our professor called the *uncommitted middle* – the fence-sitters you're attempting to peel away from your opponent.

This tension between the power of the message and blaming the messenger is tracked assiduously by political media observers and influencers (they are often one in the same). That's why planting seeds of suspicion requires the messenger to disavow all authorship. Their effectiveness is neutralized once their messages are tainted by their own self-interest. The accusations and innuendos are much more convincing when the originator of the claims is not implicated by the reporters and pundits who broker the story. All credibility is gone when the messenger becomes the message.

A skilled political operative or public relations manager keeps their fingerprints off the revelations they leak to the news media. Assuming the reporter gets the scoop they were promised, this is a better than even trade for the leaker.

Once the story is delivered, the operative retreats to the war room to watch the sparks fly, their opponents squirm, track the implications, and stay ahead of the story. Whether having gone negative inflicts more damage than it sustains, both first party sides understand the third-party public the same way. The key determinants are no different for claiming victory than they are for escaping blame:

FIGURE 4.38: Gauging Reactions to Going Negative

Determinant: What's in it for me?		->What's it gonna cost?
1. NEGATIVE:	What's being taken away from me	->Who's it being given to?
2. POSITIVE:	What's being given to me	->What's expected in return?

Here's another campaign fundamental they drill into hired guns in training: A negative that's not responded to becomes grounded. The corollary here is that a negative with grains of reality becomes gospel truth. That reality cuts deep enough to trip any get-out-the-vote drive lacing up its campaign boots. Going positive might be riskier than playing defense.

The negative message is an economizing one. An accusation lands on its target and the audience processes the remark with only one question in-mind — how will the accused respond? A positive message takes much longer to be absorbed and believed. It's a defensive impulse that predates U.S. Presidential elections, perhaps even romantic betrayals.

That's because survival trounces reality. That's because positive news forms an instant response before a question can even form. That reflex says: *what's in it for you?* What potential conflict-of-interest lies buried in that cheery delivery of my selective facts?

The Best Defense

Up until now, we've spoken of *being used* by information in passive ways. We're enchanted with our gadgets or intoxicated with the access and control they afford us. But there are also intentional efforts to distort or devalue the original context of information. They're used to compromise an informant, an investigator, or persons whose knowledge may jeopardize the security and/or mission of a first party institution. We need to diffuse these risk factors before their detonation does harm to our families and friends, as well as our stature as investigators.

The increasing connectedness of porous, virtual borders is an opportunity to explore and test those connections. It is also threatens our ability to maintain confidences and hold secrets. So too, it endangers our ability to stifle unsubstantiated rumors. It removes the former safeguard of journalists to correct factual inaccuracies or quotes that may reflect the correct wording, but not the way the subject was trying to communicate their message.

Simply put, how do we set the record straight, when there are competing versions of the same record?

Such confusions and uncertainties are breeding grounds for misinformation campaigns. The campaigners conceal their attempts to mislead, distract, or misrepresent behind a self-selecting sets of facts supported by mounting bodies of dubious evidence.

Don't Believe Everything You Think

Misinformation is not always delivered through a diabolical intention. Sometimes our own assumptions blind us to the fact we are not our own best petitioners.

The most universal form of conflict-of-interest is the edict that one cannot confer credibility onto one's self. The information provider is compromised when they are the source *and* the story. Even highly confident and ego-driven type A personalities will instinctively seek professional representation through agents and brokers. This is preferable to representing their own interests directly. Is that because they're secretly bashful?

More than likely they've come to terms with the fact that they will be seen as one-sided versions of their own world views. They will not be perceived as impartial arbiters with the broader perspective needed to reconcile their self-serving interest with a more prevailing one.

Nothing Personal

The diffusion of risk factors means keeping a vigilant but dispassionate focus on misinformation as an information source. That means tuning into potential risks without rushing to judgments, falling victim to our own protective instincts, and seeing the paranoia in others for what it is: An unflattering blend of obsession, vanity and fear.

Obsessive behavior is a temptation when under attack. But paranoia is a luxury of the self-important. Wearing one's distrust on their sleeve can easily backfire – especially when acting wounded or defensive adds merit to the claims made against us. Is our outrage fueled by our sense of justice, guilt, or fear of what's to come? It's a dilemma few of us can sustain under the glare of public scrutiny. Self-defense shows us on our guard and shows our detractors that they may have knocked us off our game. We've lost all perspective between the evidence in question and our firsthand role in shaping the perceptions of the people who were not there with us.

For now let's assume that we're not under attack. Time is on our side. We know that the misinformers may not be all that informed of their own limitations as communicators. They might not even be aggressive or hostile so much as sloppy and oblivious of any unintended consequences.

There are three ways we will approach misinformation with deliberation and transparency, not defensiveness and firewalls! Misinformation providers earn our suspicions when they...

- Pay second parties to create a sense of false trust in the expectations and beliefs of third parties.
- Perpetrate fraud by projecting a sense of authority and confidence in times of turbulence and uncertainty.
- Game systems like Google's search rankings so that the gamers appear more legitimate or credible than their track record merits.

Here's how those defenses align.

1) Paying Others to do our Bidding: The Price of Social Media Admission

Nowadays, anyone cloaked in celebrity is a potential Trojan horse for peddling ads through micro-messaging platforms like Twitter. The brokers match the endorsers with the brands that match up best with their personalities. That match is critical if an endorsement is going to ring true in their tweets as well as their relationship to their fans and followers (recipients). **(Glover, 2011)**[20] The introduction of intermediaries is the newest wrinkle in the stealth marketing efforts of popular consumer brands. It's advertisers who began the practice of creating *buzz marketing* by paying bloggers to promote their firms or products without disclosing their motives for doing so. **(Gillmor, 2009)**[21]

These examples are a complete reversal of the subscription model where recipients once paid to receive ad-supported media. The reality of social media and the collapse of second parties is that the media is no longer ad-supported. The media is the medium and that medium is advertising.

The all-volunteer cadre of editorial staffers who safeguard Wikipedia presents a more insidious form of misinformation. They remove the the first-party distortions of vanity and self-protection. Wikipedia articles have their own self-selecting treatment of the subjects they cite. For instance, the fluid and transient tastes of Wikipedia's editorial staff skews the importance of group pastimes far beyond their merit as cultural influences:

> "Popular cultural looms large. The entry for the game Halo, for example, is significantly longer than the one for the Protestant Reformation." **(Bennett, 2011)**[22]

This kind of self-identity cuts us off from divinations that run deeper than any religious sect, let alone gaming application. The immediacy of now is tyrannical. There is no longer a grace period or a honeymoon. There is no requisite down time to take in the tumult of disruptive events and accord them the proportion, connectedness, and possible redress they deserve.

To its credit, those same editors are zealous enforcers of second party filtering between message senders and recipients:

> "Thanks to WikiScanner, software that cross-references the Net contributors of contributors, watchdogs have found that computers at ExxonMobil, Pepsico, and Diebold, among others, have been used to remove unflattering information from the companies' entries."

Devised by a CalTech student named Virgil Griffith, this safeguard is very much in keeping with the same credibility scoring we used to compare first and second parties. **(Borland, 2007)**[23] In this example, we compare a first party (Wal-mart) commenting on its own controversial employee healthcare policies with those of second parties. It's in that comparison that we can not only invite conjecture about motives but quantify the gap in these two perspectives. Our PCF-based perspective focuses on the disinterested third parties who have no personal or direct experience on either side of the debate.

FIGURE 4.39: The Hows and Whys Behind Misinformation Sources

Misinformation Provider	Intent	Blindspot	Consequences	Tools / Methods
Political operative going negative	Keep independent voters at home on election day	Can't get in front of story when messenger becomes the message	Distorting attachments	Use demagoguery to create false choices and over-simplify complex issues
Financial planner games the system	Fabricate expertise to an affluent and financially illiterate clientele	Clients' investments vanish as claims of fraud and lawsuits materialize	Inappropriate self-interest	Inflated PageRank commands in search results
Cyberbully contributor to 'honest' Facebook	Catering to a credibility gap between personal proclamation and perceptions of others	Anonymous sources are free to allege and insinuate with impunity	Character assassination – civility ceases when mutual admiration is no longer reciprocated	Only paid subscribers earn the right to 'free' speech
Trojan horse ad peddlers	Use known personalities to validate faceless merchandise and services	Celebrity discovered using a competitor's product	Publicists masquerade as news reporters when third parties are looking for honest brokers	Product placements via celebrity micro-blogging
Short selling day trader	Wants to inflate shares by inviting speculations of mergers and buyouts	Market chatter is not traceable to a specific provider	Unconfirmed rumors savage the share prices of worthy stocks – most are about stock sell-offs, not deal-making	Stocks plummet the day after the rumor passes

OVERCOME BY EVENTS (AND MISINFORMANTS)

Our deadline to respond is yesterday. Other people we care about are waiting on our decision. What would our information therapist say?

The most common ways that we as recipients are overwhelmed by too much information and thus prone to misinformants is that decisions must be made within a limited period. Time pressures created by short-term decisions concerning us seem even more pressing because...

- Big issues often play out in good and bad ways, but our ignorance of them means we must assume the worst.
- We may not grasp what's good for us...
- But we surely get what's good for the competing interest that the misinformant is demonizing to *clear the air* and *set the record straight*.

Misinformation providers are bound by the following aims:

1. They want to create a sense of certainty in the minds of their recipients.
2. The issues they address are a source of unresolved anxiety.

As recipients, we feel defensive and defenseless at the same time: Defensive because we're guarding against a negative outcome. Unwelcome surprises open us up to many more sources than we feel comfortable letting in. That explains to some extent why we drink from the fire hose of the emails and texts that come crashing down in our pockets and purses. It's not because we're convinced we can stay on top of everything. It's that we don't want *everything* to climb on top of us.

The defenseless side speaks to the turns and twists taken by our worst case scenarios around money, health, love, and social standing – all the likely culprits. That's when we're most vulnerable to messages that bring order and closure to these chaotic and control-resistant events. That's when misinformation carries the argument to us. Its eloquence lies in a simplicity so persuasive that we barely need convincing.

Tools of the Misinformation Trade

That's why misinformants take aim at complex and thorny topics with sweeping and conclusive messages. Misinformation tells us what we want to hear. It simplifies the details and permits us to move on: Either in deciding on a course of action (say, hiring an expert) or deciding to stand pat (sitting out an election). Misinformation finds its mark by taking aim at us in the following ways:

1. Replaying simple arguments with a limited range of predictable outcomes
2. Offering clear alternatives with positive or at least clarifying results
3. Requiring little or no additional input from the recipient

In this section, we'll consider several specific instances of misinformation campaigns. We will see how misinformants typically feast on our own insecurities – particularly when we spread our awareness into areas that impair our judgement. Broadly speaking, here's how that plays out in popular media channels such as the high-stakes political and financial arenas:

1) Guilt by association – Fixating on a sweeping conclusion that labels all affiliated members of one group as the *same*, meaning they...

    A. Hold to the same views and protect the same interests

    B. Harbor similar resentments

    C. Play by their own self-serving justifications and disregard for rules, mainstream views, etc.

2) Cover-up by smokescreen – Creating a fuss that overshadows any harmful exposure that may come to misinformants who...

    A. Implicate an adversary or potential enemy by leaking secrets about them they won't expose (alleged cover-up)

    B. Bluff reporters into accepting unsubstantiated rumors with a *scoop* that beats other providers to the punch

    C. Force a separation to avoid an implication by distancing the provider from deviant or controversial affiliates

3) Exaggerate by staging drama – Telling a narrative grounded more on attention-getting than sense-making where storytellers...

    A. Sensationalize an otherwise dubious claim or obscure topic with celebrity references and insinuations

    B. Inflate the dimension of ongoing disputes so that honest disagreements cascade into shouting matches

    C. Raise the suspicion that if opponents emerge victorious from an initial litmus test, it will trigger an irreversible trend, act as contagion, etc.

Sources of Misinformation

Who's likeliest to be the brainchild of a misinformation campaign? Whether we're talking about Machiavellian power magnet or market manipulators, their deceptions are intended to keep them a step ahead of their victims. This strategy serves the dual purpose of dictating the terms of a debate and the flash points of the conflict. The misinformant maintains the upper hand by keeping their opponents guessing where and when they'll be forced into a response.

Here are four types of misinformation providers, and the context in which they tend to flourish:

1. **Partisans and true believers** – Look hard at the principled stances held by rigid hardliners. They may have no intention of reaching a compromise, honoring a brokered truce, or even recognizing the legitimacy of dissenting views. How do we know? They're not looking to the next legal ruling or election cycle, but to the next round of doubts fueled in a counter-punch media offensive.

2. **Self-sanctioning experts** – Ever stuck in an information mess? What if we could pay a domain expert to plow us out? It's a common assumption that well-credentialed analysts are valued for advice. But the credibility afforded by their stature provides the justification for the groups who retain them to act in their own interests. In effect, they are providing political cover as well as advice. **(Weinberg, 2009)**[24] This form of credibility for hire is fraudulent whenever their fact-base is cherry-picked by their clients to fit the picker's own pre-determined objectives.

3. **Traceless originators** – The most popular author of accusations and slanderous defamations is named Anonymous Sources. Whether Sir or Madam Anonymous goes by *high level officials* or *secret admirers,* a protected identity is the surest way to grease the communication wheels. Anonymity lowers the risks to information providers for providing false and misleading evidence and groundless speculation. Case-in-point: The surest way to play the stock market is to assume that merger rumors are wrong and bet against them. That's because they rarely pan out. Instead the takeover buzz prompts a run on these stocks. Their corrective declines are soon to follow. **(Lachapelle, 2011)**[25]

4. **Trigger-happy journalists** – Not all misinformation is malicious or innately negative. As the self-appointed timekeepers of historic import, the media is the misinformed source that rushes to report on deaths greatly exaggerated (to paraphrase Mark Twain). Think of elections not officially won, e.g. the Florida vote in the Presidential Election of 2000. In such cases, the goal to be dull and accurate is overcome in the rush to be breathless and break the story.

Scams and Frauds: Who wants to be an authority?

As we saw with in the social media instances, the web offers information providers some novel approaches for manufacturing credibility. That's especially the case when the demand is for finding experts and the supply is a surplus of web hits. Scamming is about filling in the blank formed by that top qualification factor in all public reputations: "According to _____, everything we reported yesterday is wrong, now that we know _____ ."

FIGURE 4.40: Value Proposition for Experts

```
Higher the stakes + Lower our understanding
= the greater our desperation to fill this hole
```

The gamers' intent is to...

- ■ Elevate themselves by substituting an impartial but convincing group of first parties (customers) and third-parties (experts) to sing their praises.

- ■ Denigrate a rival or raise doubts about the competition in order to profit from the confusions and speculations of customers and investors alike. The role of hedge funds in major run-ups on the price of commodities and energy sources are prime examples here.

Of course, no one's going to read every single testimonial and vet the credentials of every party that petitions on the gamers' behalf. That's why a systematic ranking is so persuasive. It rounds up all the market noise signified in all the search results to a single, identifiable action plan: *"Go with _____."* Like the t-shirt says: *How can 77,000,000 Elvis fans be wrong?*

The effort to divert collective action away from a common purpose (what's available?) towards a specific outcome (buy my product!) is hardly a new phenomenon or limited to web searches. In a market-driven economy and culture, there will always be a competitive factor that attempts to redirect or overwrite any effort to define a common interest or greater public good.

Effective issues or policy-based research is not only about providing a balanced, objective, or impartial assessment of a public concern or resource. It's about resisting the efforts of private parties to coerce or bias the outcome in their own favor.

As public trust in institutions continues to erode, so too the temptation and ability to distort the notion of what's good for most or what's great for some grows in our digital discourse. The name for this subversive act is *gaming the system.* In this case, the game is fraud, and the system for perpetrating the scam is the Internet.

For example, what do we do when we're assaulted by information, convinced we have to act on this bombardment, and not certain how? We turn to an authority. We put our trust in a source that recipients know and trust and presumably share some mutual risk and potential gain – *if my source is correct, then we both win.*

Con artists understood this long before global trading and computer networks communications made the practice widespread. The huge gains in world financial markets made at the turn of the new century convinced many that we were living in a new golden age. This was to be an age of 'Frictionless Capitalism' — a world of unlimited wealth defying the normal laws of economic gravity. Ostentatious displays of well-heeled tycoons and the new super rich feasted on the dreams and insecurities of less shrewd and/or fortunate investors. Did I miss the boat? How could I too have the Internet punch my ticket to prosperity?

FIGURE 4.41: Debunking Tool Organized by Fact-checking Authorities

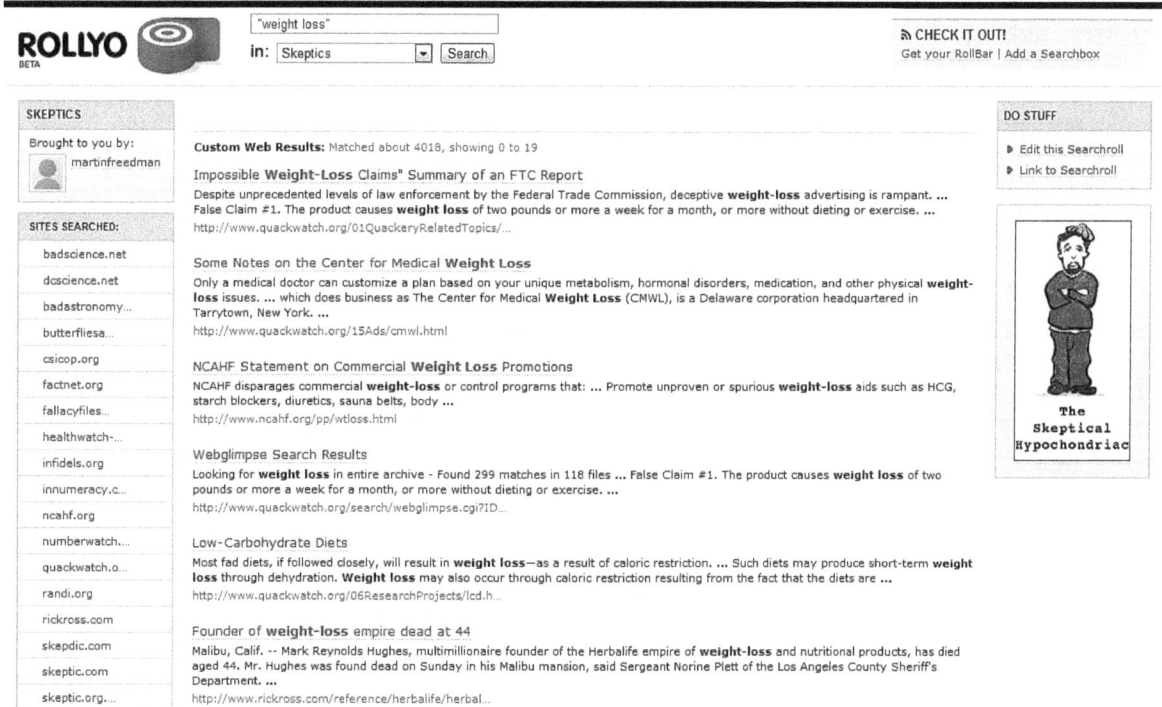

This screen capture references a search engine that combines dozens of myth-busting sites designed to set the record straight on familiar hoaxes and urban legends. This is a prime example of the OLP construct we first saw in Unit Two – in this case we're fishing in a relative pond for a well-documented fact base behind dubious claims related to dieting.

Scam Haven

Offshore islands like Swiss banks are tax havens where the powerful can shelter their incomes from the homeland authorities. The Internet is also a haven. It's not for concealing wealth but for forging identities, planting rumors, generating doubt or confusion, and most importantly, boosting the credibility of dubious groups and institutions.

How does this happen? What makes the web a haven for scams? Let's go back to a fairly common cause of information overload. No industry is capable of generating more excessive, unfiltered, and often conflicting information than the financial services industry. Indeed information is not only its primary resource but its chief by-product. After profits, the only tangible product it manufactures is ... that's right — a flood of information.

What happens when we go on overload about something that tests our understanding, and impacts us so directly? This happens when...

- We need to take action *before* we're ready.
- Dramatic shifts to the market and the stress this causes impedes our better judgment.
- We don't know much about the causes and effects of market gyrations.
- What we do know is that our reasoning abilities are compromised.
- We turn to financial experts.

What does this have to do with the web? Plenty.

Google is no more an information broker than Google is a mere search engine. It is the virtual friend and neighbor we turn to when the complexities of the world overwhelm our senses, over-match our knowledge, and even overpower the coping skills we use to handle high levels of uncertainty. Short of wishing the problem away, or reducing the confusion, is the enduring need to reach higher ground: The state of knowing when the bottom's dropped out or defining what it even looks like.

Then there's the reverse scenario. When giddy markets are buoyed by unbridled optimism. In times of prosperity, who is detached but also invested? Who can tell when soaring expectations crash past the barriers of reasonable rates of return?

What we want is a hedge against our loftiest dreams and our worst nightmares. What we want is a voice of reason. That's the persuasion that drowns out the endless sets of mediated search results and landing pages, crafted around our click histories — the messages and products we've bought before. And hearing is believing when the voice of reason doesn't come from the source. It comes from all the others who've benefited from a higher searching out loud reasoning.

Playing to the Crowd

As we know, search results include more unworthy hits than we can filter. What we can do is focus on the objective of the misinformant's deception — the third-party crowd in play for fraudulent provider.

Audience-directed praise and influence are expressed in one of two ways:

1. **Formal:** definitive endorsements based on orchestrated, fee-based campaigns through traditional advertising and media
2. **Viral:** in-process endorsements that are open to all and spontaneously formed through word-of-mouth and other free forms of expression

It is when we mistake the orchestrated campaign for the viral endorsement where the risk of fraud is greatest. Systems that create rankings or ratings through opinions and recommendations are especially prone to this kind of manipulation. Many of those impartial references are actually vested sponsors of the gamer. Sometimes, they are one in the same.

The engineering of search engine results is more than a lucrative cash cow for Google. It's the playing board on which the players (global Googlers) go to fill their gaping blanks (who gets my investment dollars). Assuming the name's familiar and the reviews are promising, the final verdict is in before the trading ticker refreshes.

These are the unregulated practices of gamers whose market fortunes rise in direct response to their search result positioning. Those are the rules to the game. And surprise ... the system is rigged. The facade of authority and the persuasion it confers is not only self-serving scheme but a self-fulfilling outcome. Appearances overwhelm reality until the bill comes due.

3) Gaming the Search System: Optimization at the Expense of Relevance

Another common form of distortion stems from feigning the popularity of websites by inflating the number of referring pages to raise a site's search position (or what Google calls its PageRank). With the emergence of search results as a marketing tool, more and more advertisers are trying to influence search terms in their favor.

Pay-per-Click (or "PPC") campaigns are an established way to achieve favorable positioning within the first set of search results. Matching a specific word or phrase they purchase from the search engine vendor promote their sites, services, and/or products. A landing page created by the advertiser either tops the results list and/or appears a noticeable area.[26]

UNIT FOUR: Sense-making Through Information Context | Page 4:101

Another way that marketers try to influence these outcomes is to bypass the search engine companies altogether. They try to artificially inflate their prominence and positioning through other means than direct advertising. This practice is referred to as search engine optimization (or "SEO").

One common SEO practice is to inflate the number of links between the pages each marketer is trying to boost in the search rankings. Sometimes this is done through reciprocal links exchanged between two cooperating entities. Other times a sole actor will artificially inflate their rankings by fabricating the popularity of their pages through a scheme called "link farms." The content of link farms is useless to anyone outside the group who creates them. Land in one and you've gotten that sinking feeling. Most of us have fallen into this familiar information ditch. The site we stumble on provides a keyword match to our concerns (and apparently everyone else's!) These sites exist for no other reason than to inflate the search ranking of the interests who generate them.

FIGURE 4.42: Carving up the First Page of Search Results (Circa 2010)

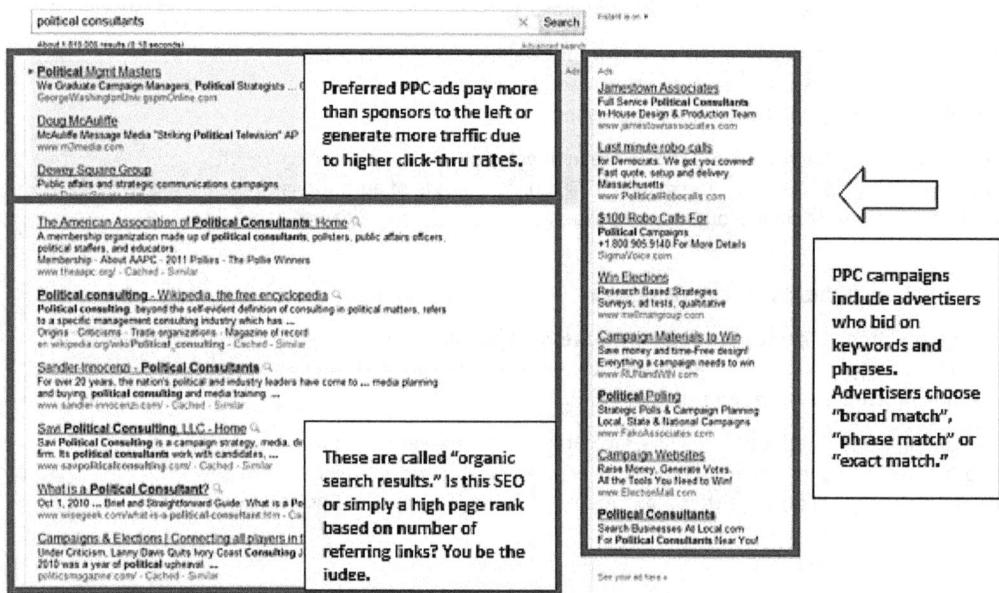

SEO is organic search – the main results that money can't buy. They represent 75% of all click-throughs. The other quarter is SEM on the right side of the screen. Many SEM click-throughs lead to landing pages (usually the ability to purchase the service advertised on the search results page).

UNIT FOUR: Sense-making Through Information Context | Page 4:102

FIGURE 4.42: Carving up the First Page of Search Results (Circa 2019)

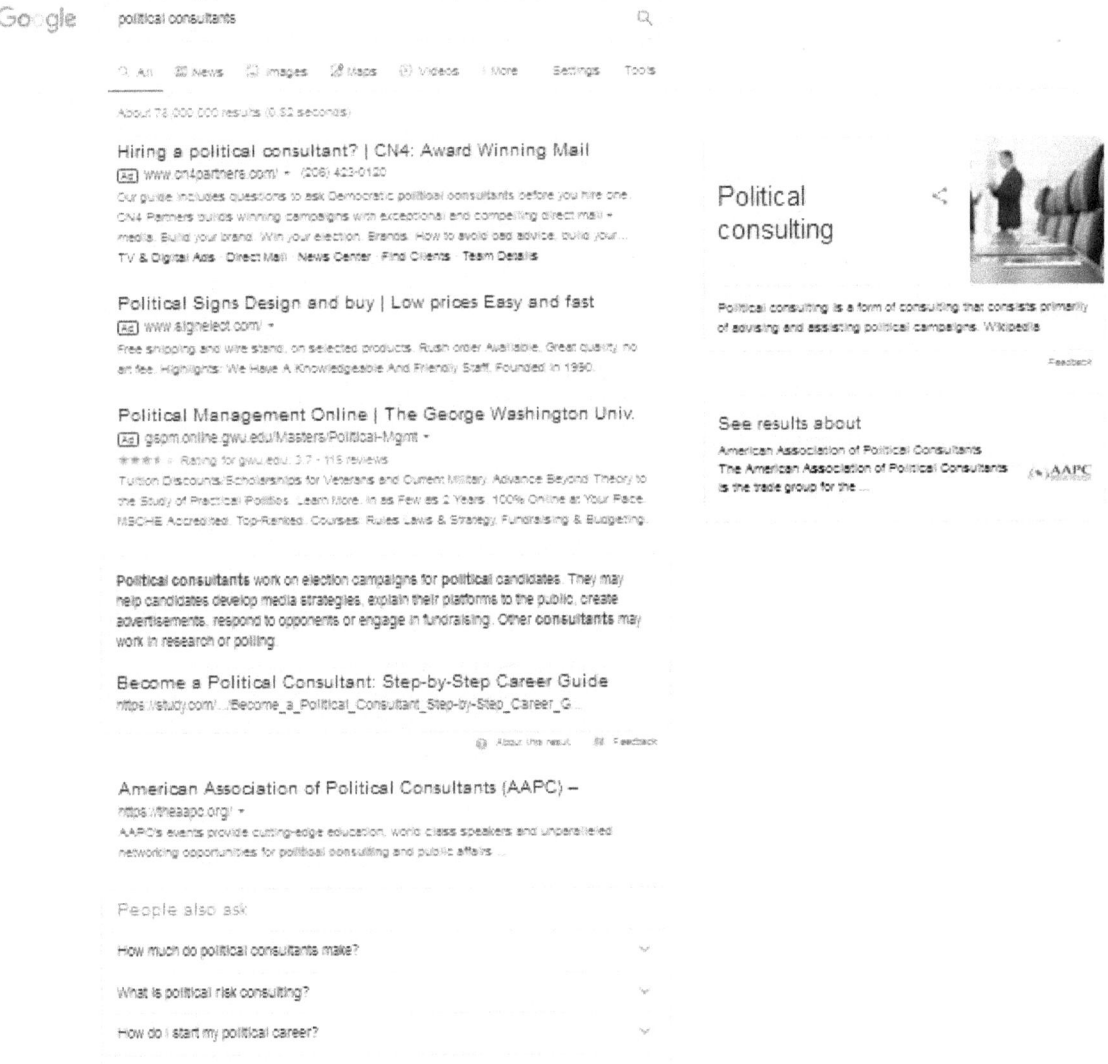

Organic search results have been reduced substantially. They've been replaced by ads now appearing in the top three slots and by the featured snippet below them. This is a text box summarizing the topic that most closely correlates to the query. Other topic-related questions are stacked below a prominent trade association – the only organic search result in this example.

Scoring Systems that Rate Themselves

Perhaps more than all the other potential conflicts-of-interest that investigators track, the outcome of gaming the system is an abuse that the digital world is well-equipped to document. After all, once news gets out, it can only travel fast. And the speed is based less on what the news is, and more about how it spreads virally – through the web like wildfire.

Contriving to win a contest by turning the rules of the game against itself is a fantasy sport witnessed firsthand in every set of returning search results. Coercive schemes like link farms exist solely of sites that link to other sites. Why? For increasing their link popularity score or PageRank in Google. Think of them as 'search spam.'

There are other ways to create false perceptions online. Much of the electronic trading done prior to the financial meltdown of 2008 concerns the fabricated credit default swaps. This is where short-sellers faked trades to incite market fears that the stocks of the companies they were selling signaled that these companies' fortunes were about to turn sour: A self-fulfilling prophesy.

Is there a role here for PCF? Can the query formation techniques that we introduced in Section 4.2 help us to make sense of system rigging?

First, we look for potentially false perceptions created by first persons or parties who manipulate scoring systems and institutional procedures to appear influential, respected, or unduly popular. Their fortunes rise in parallel with favorable search rankings or endorsed by the very rules they are trying to thwart.

This is particularly useful when we're trying to get a handle on the leading players in less established and fledgling markets. That's when we're likeliest to see a disconnect between a company's meager resources, and its formidable digital presence.

Everybody's Doing It

Another powerful use in the digital research of misinformation campaigns is to document awareness levels. Awareness could mean a lot of things from personal popularity to marketing campaigns and public policies. It is especially persuasive when we can connect awareness level to peoples' notion of choices they can take by acting on such awareness. This is not just about Coke and Pepsi or Democrats and Republicans. It's about something much more widespread and fundamental than who we vote for or even what goes in our shopping carts. It's about what's standard and what's deviant. It's about determining a normal from extreme that would otherwise go undefined.

For example, criminality is about deviance. The more prevalence we see in ruthless and self-serving behavior, the harder it is to punish someone for this kind of wrongdoing. **(Parloff, 2009)**[27] That doesn't mean that widespread brutality is an excuse for coldblooded murder. It does mean that the more commonly recognized that lying, cheating and stealing become, the more difficult it is to prosecute the guilty. This becomes important when authorities and leaders need to hold up the most egregious violators as teaching examples. The prevailing lesson here for the larger community is that such flagrant behaviors would no longer be tolerated.

In such cases it becomes essential to test some meaningful questions:

1. How widespread is the behavior?
2. Who crossed the line the most times or by the widest margin?
3. Who did it first (thus providing cover to all the subsequent copy-cats)?

Next Steps

As investigators it's a mistake to confuse disinterest with detachment. Playing the observer doesn't suggest a passive role or remaining in a reactive mode. That's when the impaired judgment rests with us and our own insecurities or haste for closure when certainty is a long way off. The better approach is to keep our sights peeled on providers and their motives for providing misinformation.

As we discussed in **Unit One,** the web is a great way to assess the social influences that surround people as search targets. From screening criminal suspects to potential hires, the web is a great way to test for blindspots and those areas most ripe for lapses in judgment. Questionable loyalties, compromised resources, and unmet obligations are all in play above our Internet radars, especially where social media is the information provider's milieu. Red flag conditions exist in all walks of commerce and levels of professional conduct. **(Campbell, Whitehead, Finkelstein, 2009)**[28]

Red Flag Conditions

What are some smoking guns? Where does our sniff test take us? Three red flags are frequently raised. The occasion? These are the most common lapses in the calculations of misinformation providers:

1. **Inappropriate self-interest —** The limits of our own personal experience prevent us from seeing how our actions impact others and their interpretations for what we do. Self-preservation erodes our ability to see our own biases, even when we petition on behalf of others. It is not by accident but design that in most high level negotiations we hire brokers to do our bidding. But when personal loyalties blind us to impartial observation, we lose the confidence of our professional peers. The *greater good* no longer prevails above the privileged concerns of the well-connected.

2. **Distorting attachments —** Personalizing adversity is an honest, authentic, and entirely human response to our own vulnerability. It is also nearly always unprofessional. Whenever we experience an emotionally-charged event, we are prone to raising the specter of that same threat in the future. Holding on to past grievances can often lead to future blunders. Instead of taking the long view, our search target fixates on some slight or wound inflicted from a feuding enemy.

3. **Misleading memories** — It's a standard assumption that someone with a track record of success is a better risk to build on that success than someone with less experience or a mixed record. The red flag rationale argues that success can breed overconfidence. If prior decisions turned out well, our target is blinded to key differences as conditions change and new conflicts arise. If the rewards of past smear campaigns eclipse the downsides, those approaches are likelier to repeat – if not the successes.

Who Fact Checks the Fact-checkers?

In the era of rapidly unfolding accusations and counter-punches comes the fact checkers. This is a research-based response to fill the vacuum formed between abject reality and the vested interests exposed in the electoral cycle. Fact-checkers scrutinize the dueling communication strategies of opposing campaigns. They are perceived to carry no personal biases and harbor or concealed motives other than (1) expand on the gap between an impartial observation, and (2) the distortions carried in campaign speeches, interviews, and news leaks.

They are sensitive to distinctions meant to objectify, marginalize, and ultimately demonize the, judgment, and character of the opposing camp. Conversely, an effective fact checker doesn't cross into the realm of advocacy. The fact checking lets the reader draw their own conclusions within the basis of facts, behavior, and perceptions evidenced by the research presented.

To the Knowledge-ABLED, this means handing over the ingredients and the recipe so that the message consumer (or voter in this case) can test *the same* set of facts. Recipients of all political stripes can dish out their own opinions — in their own kitchens.

One way to move beyond the emotional minefields of veiled threats and character assassinations is to steer clear of opinions entirely. Instead, focus on the more concrete aim of verification — specifically the degree to which evidence is being stretched to support the bias of the candidate. For instance, economic trends that underpin the policy changes favored by the campaign may align with a longstanding trend that's slowing, dormant, or even reversing in recent surveys. Another hotbed for skepticism is that the underlying logic of an argument is based on a faulty set of assumptions, or a choice of misleading comparisons. **(Kessler, 2016)**[29]

THE DUBIOUS FREEDOM OF ANONYMOUS SPEECH

One of the freedoms of a virtual world is that we get to play act or try out different sets of identities, based on the way we portray ourselves in simulated environments. We can try on new attitudes or assume personality traits and behaviors that are quite apart from our real-world identities and circumstances. That escapism is encouraged by the widespread use of 'handles' or so-called sock puppets — pseudonyms that shield recipients from knowing our contact information.

The liberation from our legal identities and actual places can also remove our sense of personal responsibility and fair play when we assume the role of information provider with impunity. There are no consequences for unfounded criticisms we find easier to make under the cover of an alternative and anonymous identity. The allure of a rich fantasy life masks the drudgery and unglamorous nature of daily existence. But it also confuses the balance between providing information and being accountable for the evidential details we share.

UNIT FOUR: WRAPPING

FOCUSING ON INFORMATION CONTEXT

Unit Four transitioned our Knowledge-ABLED approach to investigations from the usage phase of our research-gathering to the interpretive stages of our own weighing of the evidence. While **Unit Three** addressed the motives of information givers, **Unit Four** wrestled with the contextual merits of our evaluations process. We did this by focusing on follow-up actions and outcomes – namely how individual and group stakeholders process the digital content they both consume and produce through social media. Throughout this unit, we assessed how those deliberations should factor into our own analysis. **Unit Five** will square the substance of our research with the packaging and style requirements for best presenting these findings to our peers, clients, and stakeholders. Those presentation methods are critical, not just to our credibility as investigators, but as trusted advisers. Ultimately we are judged not by our findings, but by the recommendations we draw from our research.

[1] Kevin Maney, "The Ratings Game," The Atlantic, July, 2009
[2] Pennabaker, Chung, "Computerized Text Analysis," January, 2007
[3] Carl Elliot, "The Ghostwriter," The Atlantic Monthly, December, 2010
[4] Muhammad Farhan, "Cnewsworld, WikiLeaks Diplomatic Disclosures Cover all Full Report," December, 1, 2010
[5] An expression attributed to Edward de Bono, a psychologist, physician and writer.
[6] David Frum, "Severely Conservative?" The Daily Beast, February 10, 2012
[7] University of Oregon psychologist Paul Slovic conducted an experiment. He told undergraduates about a starving child named Rokia -- she lived in a crumbling refugee camp in Africa. His students expressed their sympathy with an outpouring of about $2.50 to a well-known charity. However, when it was communicated to a separate student group that over five million African children are malnourished -- the average donation dipped by half.
[8] Ronald Heifetz, The Practice of Adaptive Leadership, Harvard Business, 2009
[9] Professor Tannen remarks that news coverage of global warming actually ends up being biased because news reports of scientists' mounting concern typically also feature

prominently one of the few "greenhouse skeptics" who declare the concern bogus. This "balanced" two-sides approach gives the impression that scientists are evenly divided, whereas in fact the vast majority agree that the dangers of global climate change are potentially grave.

[10] Michael Lewis, David Einhorn, "The End of the Financial World as We Know It," The New York Times, January 4, 2009

[11] Charles Arthur, "Analysing data is the future for journalists, says Tim Berners-Lee," The Guardian, November 22, 2010

[12] Not all information sources within group circle consist of multiple persons. Sometimes a single individual may be responsible for speaking for a group, as is the case with corporate executives, elected officials, tribal elders, or even celebrities.

[13] Josh Tyrangiel, "2010 in Review," Businessweek, December 20, 2010

[14] The real payoff is that they are now free to speak their minds without the constraint of needing to speak on behalf of their former organization. If this blending of credibility and authenticity sounds familiar, it will ring more true the next time we reference the Vectors of Integrity from the prior section in this unit.

[15] Dan Gillmor interviewed by Brooke Gladstone, NPR's On the Media, November 19, 2010

[16] Marc Prensky, "Digital Natives, Digital Immigrants, On the Horizon," MCB University Press, Vol. 9 No. 5, October 2001

[17] Ben Zimmer, "Nominations for American Dialect Society Word of the Year, 2009," http://www.americandialect.org/Zimmer-2009-WOTY.pdf

[18] Premack, D. & Woodruff, G., "Does the Chimpanzee Have a Theory of Mind?" Behav. Brain Sc., 4, 515-526, 1978

[19] The term 'pre-teen' had not yet been coined in 1981.

[20] Ronald Glover, "And Now a Tweet from Our Sponsor," Businessweek, January 10, 2011

[21] Dan Gillmor, "Principles of a New Media Literacy," http://publius.cc/principles_new_media_literacy

[22] Drake Bennett, "Ten Years of Remarkable Detail: Wikipedia," Businessweek, January 10, 2011

[23] John Borland, "See Who's Editing Wikipedia - Diebold, the CIA, a Campaign," Wired Magazine, August 14, 2007

[24] David Weinberg, "Your Help with the New Expertise," KM World, August, 2009

[25] Tara Lachapelle, "A Winning Stock Strategy: Sell on the Rumor," Businessweek, January 13, 2011

[26] Advertiser positionig has changed over the years. What was formerly on the right-side of the results page has been made increasingly prominent. Sponsored links are located directly below the search box at the time of this writing.

[27] Roger Parloff, "Wall Street: It's Payback Time," Fortune Magazine, January 6, 2009

[28] Andrew Campbell, Jo Whitehead, Sidney Finkelstein, "Think Again: Why Good Leaders Make Bad Decisions," Harvard Business Review, May, 2009

[29] Glenn Kessler, "Here Are the Facts Behind that '79 Cent' Pay Gap Factoid," Washington Post, April 14, 2016

About the Author

Marc Solomon has been a knowledge architect, search manager, and competitive intelligence director in the acronym-laced world of strategic consulting (PwC, PRTM, FSG, and FIND/SVP) as well as tech services (BellSouth, Avid Technology, and Hyperion Solutions).

He currently works in the office of the CTO at The Hartford insurance company. He's presented on search, metadata, taxonomy, and Knowledge-ABLED practices through the Boston KM Forum, Enterprise Search Summit, Gilbane, and SIKM (Systems Integrators KM Leaders).

From 2005 to 2010 he was an adjunct professor in Boston University's Professional Investigation Program where he trained budding PIs on using the web to crack criminal cases, including instruction in digital media research and information literacy.

Mr. Solomon is a contributing columnist to several trade magazines on enterprise knowledge tools, practices and business cases including Searcher, Baseline, and KM World where he contributed a year-long "reality series" of SharePoint case deployment profiles. Solomon has addressed the realities of day-to-day content management as an expert blogger in the AIIM SharePoint Community. As a search expert and knowledge guru, he has decades of experience in teaching students how to become more information literate.

Most recently he launched an Open Source Intelligence (OSINT) program at the Montague Book Mill for mid-career professionals as founder of the Society for Useful Information, whose mission is to improve the quality of digital literacy and research practices throughout Western New England.

Solomon holds a BA in the History of Technology from Hampshire College and a Masters in Professional Studies from the Graduate School of Political Management at George Washington University. He lives with his wife Patty, Jaspurr the cat, and occasionally their three grown children in a home with no smart speakers and where no one searches in silence.

www.ingramcontent.com/pod-product-compliance
Lightning Source LLC
Chambersburg PA
CBHW081324040426
42453CB00013B/2293